W9-ACN-986

6.95

The Canoe

AN ILLUSTRATED HISTORY

Give me of your bark, O Birch-tree!
Of your yellow bark, O Birch-tree!
Growing by the rushing river,
Tall and stately in the valley!
I a light canoe will build me,
Build a swift Cheemaun for sailing,
That shall float on the river,
Like a yellow leaf in Autumn,
Like a yellow water-lily!

The Song of Hiawatha
Henry Wadsworth Longfellow

The Canoe

AN ILLUSTRATED HISTORY

Jim Poling, Sr.

The Countryman Press
Woodstock, Vermont

Copyright © 2000 by Jim Poling, Sr.

All rights reserved. No part of this book may be reproduced in any form or by any electronic or
mechanical means, including information storage and retrieval systems, without permission in
writing from the publisher, except by a reviewer, who may quote brief passages.

Library of Congress Cataloging-in-Publication Data
Poling, Jim, Sr.
The canoe : an illustrated history / Jim Poling, Sr.
p.   cm.
ISBN 0-88150-503-X (alk. paper)
1.   Canoes and canoeing--History. 2. Indians of North America--Boats. I. Title.
E98.C2 P65 2001
797.1'22'09--dc21   00-064508

Front cover photograph by Rolf Kraiker
Design by Peter Maher

Photo credits: CP Archives: 22, 43, 65, 66, 98, 105, 135; National Archives of Canada: 27, 34, 51, 69, 71,
79; National Gallery of Canada: 106; Rolf Kraiker: 3, 6, 9, 11, 25, 56, 74, 88, 100, 116, 119, 121, 125,
126, 129, 130, 132, 135, 136, 137, 139; The Mariner's Museum, Virginia: 111; The McMichael Gallery: 49,
109; Canadian Museum of Civilization: 15, 21, 85; Glenbow Archives: 2, 16, 18, 20, 31, 32, 35, 36, 40,
47, 48, 52, 54, 55, 64, 76, 81, 83, 91, 95, 96, 108, 113; Harry M. Walker: 103; U.S. National Archives:
72; National Museum of American Art, Washington, D.C./Art Resource, NY: 107; Ralph LaPlant: 38;
Roger McGregor, Ivy Lea, Ontario: 97; Old Town Canoe Company: 97; The Canadian Canoe Museum:
1, 58; The Canadian Embassy, Washington, D.C.: 102.

Published by The Countryman Press
P.O. Box 748
Woodstock, VT 05091

Distributed by W. W. Norton & Company, Inc.
500 Fifth Avenue
New York, NY 10110

Copublished in Canada by Key Porter Books Limited

Printed in Spain

10 9 8 7 6 5 4 3 2 1

C O N T E N T S

INTRODUCTION

Imagine yourself on a wilderness portage, perhaps in Minnesota or Maine, northern Ontario or the Northwest mountain country. Find a log and sit. Lean your head against a tree trunk and absorb the silence that is the keeper of the past. Close your eyes and let your imagination drift far back to other times. Can you see down the portage to the trailhead, where a man has just arrived? He is Anishinabe (Ojibwa), a North American Indian, and is bent on one knee beside the flat blue waters of the lake. Next to him is a canoe made of fresh birch bark sewn with spruce roots and caulked with pine pitch. He nudges its bow into the water and removes from his deerskin pouch a pinch of crushed tobacco leaf. He scatters the semma onto the water, looks to the sky and prays:

Gchi miigwech Gzhemnidoo. Kina gegoo emiizhyang.
Miinwa ngoding gii-giizhaak. Giizis gii binaabia.

The tobacco is an offering, his prayer a thanks to the Great Spirit for the rising sun bringing another day. He prays thanks for the gift of trees, which provided the materials he needed to make this useful and beautiful watercraft.

Perhaps you see others on the portage: a man in ancient European dress carrying an astrolabe, a primitive navigation aid; stocky young men wearing coarse shirts and colorful waist sashes hoisting much larger birch-bark canoes. Perhaps you see yourself, or someone like you, accompanied by a spouse and two school-age children. They are a family on summer vacation and they paddle away from the portage in a bright red canoe that, although made of modern synthetics, is the same basic design as the one built by the Anishinabe man.

These images illustrate the evolution of the deep relationship between North Americans and the canoe, a relationship that began with the First Peoples' need to traverse the continent's myriad lakes and streams. It is a relationship that grew through exploration, trade, settlement, and war and continues with the popularity of recreational and competitive canoeing and kayaking. The popularity has spread around the globe, with canoe societies and associations in the British Isles, across Europe, and stretching on to Far East countries such as Korea and Japan.

From the very beginning until today, the canoe has been as much an expression of freedom as a mode of water transport. Before they invented it, the First Peoples of the North American forests traveled only as far as their feet

could carry them. The canoe freed them from their immediate surroundings, opening new vistas and other hunting and gathering grounds, and thus improving their lives. They were set free of the restrictions of rocks, trees, and swamps.

Many early peoples invented different forms of the canoe. The Caribs of the Caribbean had dugouts. The Polynesians, starting as early as 2500 BC, explored and populated the South Pacific in canoes, some of which were double-hulled. The Vikings used wooden canoes before they built the larger ships that carried them across the North Atlantic. But it is the distinct North American canoe, afloat in symbolism that is almost spiritual, that has achieved global fame. The North American canoe is a brilliant blending of function and art, as elegant as it is practical. It is an expression of the skills and art of its builder.

On the water, in the hands of an expert, it is as joyful and peaceful to watch as an eagle manipulating its flight feathers against air currents. Its passage is like a fine poem recited on a quiet day.

The canoe today is much the same as it was centuries ago. The only improvements are in modern materials, and aside from durability, that improvement is questionable. Anyone who has paddled a birch-bark canoe knows that no other can match the way it kisses the water.

The canoe remains an expression of freedom. Millions of people around the world today enjoy canoeing. It lets them experience the outdoors as the Aboriginal peoples did and to slip free of the increasing complexities of modern living. When they set paddle to water, they enter a different world, a special place of beauty, tranquility, and freedom.

Pierre Elliott Trudeau, former prime minister of Canada, is the quintessential canoeist. He once explained the joy of canoeing this way:

> What sets a canoeing expedition apart is that it purifies you more rapidly and inescapably than any other. Travel a thousand miles by train and you are a brute; pedal five hundred miles on a bicycle and you remain basically bourgeois; paddle a hundred miles in a canoe and you are already a child of nature.

The canoe is a gift filled with other gifts. It is a gift of freedom to explore. A gift of understanding nature and one's place in it. It is a gift of traditions passed from one generation to the next. It is a gift of the Gzhemnidoo, Great Spirit in the language spoken by the Ojibwa, who were among the best of the birch-bark canoe builders. Anyone who has paddled silently away from the madness of modern life and into the morning mist on a faraway lake knows the greatness of the gift.

Sigurd F. Olson, the renowned Minnesota conservationist, knew the greatness of the gift and explained it in *The Singing Wilderness*:

> The movement of a canoe is like a reed in the wind.
> Silence is part of it, and the sounds of lapping water, bird songs, and wind in the trees. It is part of the medium through which it floats, the sky, the water, the shores . . . There is magic in the feel of a paddle and the movement of a canoe, a magic compounded of distance, adventure, solitude, and peace. The way of a canoe is the way of the wilderness, and of a freedom almost forgotten. It is an antidote to insecurity, the open door to waterways of ages past and a way of life with profound and abiding satisfactions. When a man is part of his canoe, he is part of all that canoes have ever known.

1

THE FIRST
CANOEISTS

When you live beside water, there is an urge, often a need, to cross it. Many a child growing up by water and woods has straddled a floating log and propelled it by hand paddling. What child hasn't taken a piece of bark or a stick and floated it across a puddle or pond? Perhaps from such simple acts canoes were born.

There had to be more than one birthplace and more than one inventor, because canoelike vessels developed independently in separate regions of the world. In North America alone, the canoe took the form of the skin-covered Arctic kayak, the bark canoe of the east-central forests, the cedar canoes of the Pacific Northwest, and the simple dugout of the Caribbean.

People of the West Indies used a word that sounded like canoe to describe a log modified for water transport. The

Arawaks hollowed and shaped large tree trunks into vessels for inter-island travel. They called them canaoua, which Christopher Columbus shortened to canoa in Spanish. The French, who later became the first European masters of the North American canoe, used the word canot, then canöe. Columbus described Carib dugouts in a letter about his first voyage in 1492–93: "They are not so wide because they are made of a single log of timber, but a galley could not keep up with them in rowing for their motion is a thing beyond belief."

A floating log no doubt was its earliest form. From there, thousands of years of experimentation and modification developed the canoe into one of the most ingenious and useful human inventions. The first modification was to permit the riding of a floating log without getting wet, or being stung, bitten, or eaten by water critters. The straightforward but hard labor of hollowing a log's topside provided a place to sit and to store rudimentary hunting and fishing equipment. Rough hand tools and controlled fire were used to burn and chip out the hollow. It was tedious work, but it produced a dugout that kept the operator relatively safe and above the surface of the water.

Dugouts were bulky and heavy to move off the water. Early forms had limited carrying capacity, but their drawbacks were offset by durability. Hitting a rock usually produced a simple dent in the wood, not a breach resulting in disastrous flooding. Durability meant the owner did not have to carve a dugout every year.

Logs dug out and shaped with crude hand tools were among the earliest canoes. They were used extensively in areas lacking the large trees needed for bark covering. This Iroquois dugout is from the Six Nations Reserve in southern Ontario circa 1912.

The Pacific Canoes

They might appear to be the crudest form of water transport, but some dugouts are an art form. On North America's Northwest Coast, where native people live among giant red cedars, dugouts were developed to their highest levels of beauty and performance. Not simply scooped-out tree trunks, they were sculpted trees intricately designed for speed and safe handling on big seas beyond sight of land. The carver had a vision of the canoe shape living inside the tree, and he sculpted until that vision was realized.

Many West Coast natives, hemmed in by mountain walls anchored in the ocean's edge, were forced to travel by canoe, and the red cedar dugout was among the most popular. Sizes varied. Hunting canoes to carry one or two men ran no more than 17 feet (5 m) in length. Larger canoes were 40 to 60 feet (12 to 18 m) long, 6½ feet (2 m) wide, and 3 feet (1 m) deep. The big canoes could carry up to two metric tons of cargo.

The great canoes of the Northwest were found, and can be found today, in the region stretching from southern Alaska down to the northwest corner of Washington State and Puget Sound. This is the land of the Tlingit, Tsimshian, Haida, Kwakiutl, Bella Coola, Nootka, and Coast Salish. These people are famous for their excellence as artist-carver-builders. They used canoes for river fishing, hunting sea

West Coast Indians sometimes used sails to power their beautifully carved canoes. Whether the sail was adopted from the Europeans or used before European contact is a matter of debate. These are Kwakiutl canoes, photographed by Edward S. Curtis in 1914. Curtis was an American photographer who traveled the western U.S. and British Columbia between 1906 and 1927 capturing on film the vanishing North American Indian cultures.

mammals on the ocean, traveling between tribes, and making war. Decorated canoes filled with celebrants dressed in red, white, and black tunics of cedar cloth and artful hats were a spectacular sight as they approached a beach for a potlatch celebration or to pick up a bride. War canoes carried high shields with loopholes through which bowmen could fire arrows.

The most familiar canoes are those of the high bows and sterns arching over the water, the trademarks of the Tsimshian, Kwakiutl, Haida, and Bella Coola. Others, made by the Nootka and Salish, had projecting bows but straight, vertical sterns. In contrast, the Musqueam built shallow canoes, mainly for river use, while the Haida deep canoes were ocean-going and considered a valuable trade commodity.

Ocean canoes allowed the First Peoples to venture out to whale territory. Juan Bodega y Quadra, Spanish sailing master and a commissioner to the Pacific West Coast, wrote in 1792 of seeing dugouts that could travel 16 leagues (close to 50 miles or 80 km) in a day. Typically, a whaling canoe carried a crew of eight. Design was critical: the craft had to be able to withstand rough seas, yet be fast enough to overtake and run alongside a whale. A harpooner sat at the bow with a weapon of yew wood. Sharp mussel shell gummed between two elk-antler barbs made up the killing head, which was detachable and tied to spruce-root rope leading to inflated sealskin floats.

The canoe ran beside the whale as the harpooner plunged in his weapon. It was a wild and dangerous enterprise. The hunters needed perfect timing and the highest degree of skill in using their crude equipment. The

Dugout canoes allowed West Coast Indians to gather food from the ocean and the rivers flowing into it. They also provided a way of moving along the coast without having to penetrate the rugged coastal mountains. This Edward S. Curtis photograph from 1915 shows a Nootka man hunting sea otters from his canoe.

paddlers had to know exactly when to sheer off as the harpoon struck, because the tail of a thrashing whale could crush a canoe like a wood shaving. They needed keen instincts for reading water and for knowing when to drive their paddles hard and when to lay off. The speed that their canoes developed came from their narrow hull designs, which also reduced stability and increased the risk of capsizing. Bladders or sealskin buoys attached to the canoe sides helped prevent rollovers or swamping in heavy seas.

Working with cedar—carving canoes, paddles, masks, and totems—was a sacred art. Selecting a tree took time and sometimes involved journeys far back into the rain forest, although the preference was to find trees close to water. Trees were judged for length and straightness, and tapped to test the quality of the heartwood. Felling the tree with crude hand tools was a momentous achievement.

"Do not fall too heavily, else you, great magician, will be broken," prayed the axmen.

Carving of shape began in the forest, lessening the weight that had to be dragged to the closest water for floating to the village. It took three to four weeks to build a canoe, and complicated rituals were involved, including prayer and sexual abstinence. Stone hammers, chisels, and adzes were the primary tools until the Europeans brought metal implements.

Once a cavity was carved, it was filled with water and hot stones to create a steam-softening stretching process. Wooden thwarts were forced between the sides to keep them stretched while the hull cooled. This forcing also raised the ends, where separately carved bow and stern pieces were fitted and held in place with dowels. Carvers then sanded the hull, which had a chipped look from shaping with hand tools, with fine sandstones and sharkskin to reduce hull drag. The outside was charred with fire to prevent sun rents and insect damage, then rubbed with fish oil as a preservative. Interiors were painted—red the favored color—with paint made of urine, resin, and oil.

The beauty of the Pacific Coast canoes was in their lines and elaborate carvings of figures representing the crests of the owner. Paddles too were works of art. They had a T-shaped crutch top and were painted with the designs of animals. Nootka paddles sometimes had a 6-inch (15 cm) spur on the bottom that allowed water to drip quietly so as not to disturb a dozing whale. Paddles with sharpened tips were used as weapons in canoe warfare.

Dugout canoes also were widely used throughout middle America, where bark was not suitable for canoe building.

Native people often combined fire with hand tools to hollow out logs for dugout canoes. These Tsimshian people of the Pacific Northwest are burning out a log's interior to construct a large canoe.

The Nez Percé and other tribes hollowed large trees by using fire and crude tools. The dugout was an important vessel for fur traders and expeditions such as the Lewis and Clark Corps of Discovery, formed by President Thomas Jefferson in 1804 to explore the American West.

The Bark Canoe

How the woodland Indians invented the much more intricate bark-skin canoe is a matter of speculation. Perhaps a child playing in the woods centuries ago found a piece of bark blown loose from a tree. The child folded its ends and then stuck them together with tree sap. He placed it into the eddy of a stream and watched it float away.

The people who occupied the deciduous forests of what

became southern Canada and the northern United States used bark to create vessels for gathering maple sap and berries. Waterproof bark cooking pots were used to boil meat when red-hot rocks were added to the water. The process for making baskets and pots was similar to that used in canoe building: seams created by folding the bark were sewn with thin, stringy roots and sealed with tree sap.

The North American natives were not the only people living in forested areas who used bark in building watercraft. Nowhere else was the bark canoe more highly evolved, however, and the birch-bark canoe was the epitome of its development. The wonder is how a Stone Age people brought it to such a high level of functionality. Decades and decades of experimentation were needed to develop a craft with low displacement yet the stability to prevent it from rolling over with the slightest movement.

Bark canoe designs varied, even among individual tribes. Canoes with high, curled ends often were built to cut through rough water on lakes or in river rapids. Decoration beneath the gunwales was scraped into the bark and sometimes painted.

Bark canoes were built by shaping the bark within stakes driven into the ground. A wooden framework was placed inside the bark skin. This Montagnais canoe-building scene at Murray Bay, Quebec, was captured in 1863 by Alexander Henderson.

Canoe building was done by eye, and knowledge gained from each canoe rested with the builders. There were no written records, no templates, except some crude measuring sticks. Considering the clumsiness of stone tools, it was impossible to build two canoes exactly alike. Metal tools became available in the middle of the sixteenth century, easing and speeding the work of carving and shaping the framework, but the individual pieces of bark and individual building-bed layouts made each canoe one of a kind. Probably the greatest praise for the Indian canoe is that the early Europeans with their knowledge, sophistication, and tools contributed nothing that improved the design or functionality.

Canoes were built from all kinds of bark, including elm, hickory, spruce, and cedar. Barks other than birch had rough surfaces and were difficult to take in large pieces. Iroquois elm-bark canoes contained several or more pieces, therefore had more seams to waterproof and were inferior to those of the Algonquian linguistic tribes such as the Ojibwa, Algonquin, Cree, and Mi'kmaq.

Birch was the perfect material. It is light, smooth, resilient, and waterproof, yet relatively tough. It was plentiful, once widely distributed across the Canadian Maritimes and northern New England and through Quebec, Ontario, Wisconsin, and Minnesota. Before the industrialization of the continent, huge stands of birch contained trees that grew 40 to 50 feet (12 to 15 m) tall, sometimes up to 80 feet (24 m), and with girths that no man could wrap his arms around. Aside from being so functional, birch bark is beautiful. Its fragile chalky white outer skin with the dark horizontal lines provides a color contrast that has been painted thousands of times in forest scenes. Its tough but pliant tan underbark can be painted or scored to create decorative baskets or other simple works of art.

To the First Peoples, the birch tree truly was a great gift from the Gzhemnidoo. It not only provided bark for canoes, but its fine-grained, hard wood was used for making toboggans, snowshoes, and utensils. The bark was the chief covering for winter wigwams and often provided rough, temporary raincoats. The tree gave torch tinder, wrapping for preserving food and medicine, animal calls, arrows, and quivers, plus medicines for coughs and for blood purification. The Penobscot of the northeast U.S. made a birch-bark ball and triangle game for their children, and Ojibwa women made birch-bark cutouts for amusement and for use in beadwork design.

The canoe was by far the most complicated use of the birch tree. Construction involved building a bark envelope into which a light wooden frame was set. The process appeared backwards to European boat builders, who first built a frame and then covered it. The Indians knew it was easier to fit a frame to a bark skin than vice versa.

Key to construction were two inner gunwale strips running bow to stern, lashed at their ends, and spread open by thwarts. This provided the longitudinal strength of the frame. When the folded bark was sewn to the gunwales, thin planking on the inside was held in place by U-shaped ribs forced into the gunwales. The pressure of the ribs pushed the planking against the bark, creating shape and adding the horizontal strength.

Construction of a birch-bark canoe took roughly two weeks of work by a man and a woman. Often canoe building was a community project and went much faster. The first chore was to walk the late-winter woods in search of a paper-birch tree large enough to provide a single sheet of bark for one canoe. A piece of at least 18 feet (5.4 m) and 4 feet (1.2 m) in circumference was needed, and only the larger trees could provide it. Tops with branches were useless, as were the bottoms, still soaked and marred by snow. The outer bark was examined for knots or weaknesses that might develop into holes. Strong bark, clear of deep blemishes and slightly less than one-quarter of an inch (0.6 cm) thick, was sought. Bark was taken in spring or early summer, when it was most easily removed. One vertical and two girdling horizontal cuts were made, and bone tools were used to pry and peel the bark sheet from its inner layer.

If a tree had to be felled, mud or clay was pasted above the chopping area and a fire was built at the base of the trunk. Charring from the fire made chopping easier while the mud shield prevented the bark from burning higher up. Once the bark was removed, it was carefully rolled inside out and carried back to camp. There it was weighted with rocks in a stream or lake, where the wetness would keep it soft.

Other building materials—gunwales, ribs, and thin sheathing—came from cedar or black spruce trees. Thwarts were carved from birch, hard maple, or ash. In the meantime there was the dirty work of gathering other materials. Long strands of root the diameter of a pencil were dug from the soil at the base of spruce trees. They were cleaned and coiled for later use. Spruce gum was scraped from the trees into birch-bark boxes. If enough could not be obtained by scraping, then the spruce trees were cut to bleed into birch-cone collectors. Ribs were split with a curved "crooked" knife, each end product roughly 5 feet (1.5 m) long, 2 inches (5 cm) wide, and one-quarter of an inch (0.6 cm) thick. They were dunked in boiling water to make them easier to shape into a U, then hung in the sun to dry. Long pieces of thin cedar sheathing were cut and set aside.

Birch trees that grew 40 to 50 feet (12 to 15 m) tall provided the skin for birch-bark canoes. The trees were found throughout New England and the Maritimes, central Canada and through to Wisconsin and Minnesota. Birches large enough for building the canoes of the past are hard to find now.

Building the Canoe

Actual building began with careful site preparation. It had to be on smooth, firm soil free of rock so stakes could be driven. The building bed was built up an inch (2.5 cm) higher than the ground surrounding it to ensure a straight bottom for the canoe. Two 17-foot (5.1 m) pieces of cedar roughly 1½ inches (3.75 cm) square were lashed together at each end to provide the start of a gunwale frame. Temporary crosspieces spread the gunwales apart. This frame was set onto the building bed and staked into shape. Once the builder was satisfied with the shape, he removed the stakes and carefully placed them beside their holes.

Next, the builder retrieved the bark from the water and rolled it onto the building bed, white side up. He placed the gunwale frame on the bark, weighting it with stones. Lifting the edges of the bark exposed the stake holes, and the stakes were driven again, holding the bark in place. Women cut and sewed the bark shell into the rough outline of a canoe. Flint knives, bone awls, and drills were used for cutting and punching holes for sewing the spruce roots that had been carefully split into half rounds with fingernails and teeth. Stitching was a matter of personal preference and pride. It could be simple or elaborate to the point of decorative.

"The Indians make no use of nails and screws but everything is sewn and tied together," Thomas McKenney, a U.S. treaty

Native women stitch strands of tree
root into this birch-bark canoe being
built on Lake of the Woods, along
the U.S.–Canada border, in 1872.
The photo was taken by an
unidentified member of the Royal
Engineers who served with the North
American Boundary Commission,
1872–75.

commissioner reported during a visit to Madeline Island,
Wisconsin, during the 1800s. "But the seams, stitches and knots
are so regular, firm and artistic that nothing better could be
asked for."

The canoe is widest at its center, so at that point the bark did not
rise as high as at the bow and stern. Bark panels were added to bring
the shell up to gunwale level. That's why in most pictures of birch-bark
canoes you see a caulked horizontal seam just below the gunwale.

The next step was to lift the building frame inside the bark shell to gunwale level. Long cedar strips were added as outside gunwales, sandwiching the top of the bark against the inside gunwale. The bark was then lashed to the wood. Many bark canoes of later origin had wooden gunwale caps that protected the root stitching against wear.

At this point the shell was rigid enough to be removed from between the stakes. Bow and stern stem pieces, bent to give the canoe its turned-up-ends shape, were lashed into place with strips of hide. The bark was trimmed to the shape and the stem pieces were sewn into position. The basic canoe was complete, except for sheathing and ribs that would give it final shape and strength.

Strips of cedar sheathing were laid lengthwise on the inside bottom of the canoe; the ends were wedged between the stem pieces and the bark. Ribs were trimmed to fit and tapped until their ends wedged under each gunwale. The ribs held the sheathing in place and forced the pliable bark to stretch and give the craft its final form. Basically, what the builders created was a vessel held together by the tension placed on its bark shell from the inside.

Seams were waterproofed with spruce gum. Gobs of it were placed in a sealed bark basket with holes in the bottom, which was lowered into hot water. The hot water separated dirt and pieces of bark from the gum, which seeped through the holes and floated to the surface. It was skimmed and mixed with a bit of animal fat to make it less brittle when it dried. Sometimes charcoal was mixed with the gum to help it set, and that gave a blacker color to the seams.

The traditional bark canoe was just over 14 feet (4.2 m) long and weighed less than 50 pounds (23 kg), although some were later built as long as 46 feet (13.8 m) for the fur trade. It was easily portaged by any adult, and despite the lightness of its materials was amazingly strong. In encounters with rocks, logs, and other underwater objects it was fragile, but this was well compensated for by ease of repair. A damaged hull was quickly fixed with a walk into the forest to collect a piece of bark, spruce-roots thread, and tree gum.

A young army cadet in Benedict Arnold's 1775 expedition to attack Quebec wrote about repairing damaged bark canoes. Cadet John Joseph Henry was part of a reconnaissance mission paddling north through Maine when their birch-bark canoe hit the branch of a fallen tree.

> One of the prongs took the right hand side of the canoe immediately below the gunwale. Quick as lightning that side of the canoe was laid open from stem to stern, and water was gushing in upon us that would have inevitably sunk us in a second of time.

They did make shore and their canoe guide showed them

how to gather bark, roots, and pitch to make the repair. No sooner was the canoe back in the water than they hit a snag and holed it again. The repairs were repeated.

The marvel of the bark canoe was its light weight compared with its large carrying capacity. It could be fully loaded and still navigate shallow water. It was ideal for the shallow streams and shoal-filled lakes of the northern woodlands. The buoyancy of the bark canoe is illustrated in a 1913 photo of 13 Ojibwa in a 19-foot (5.75 m) birch-bark canoe. Despite all that weight, 4 to 6 inches (10 to 15 cm) of freeboard are showing.

Canoes needed in a hurry could be thrown together in a few hours with whatever bark was available. Early missionaries reported seeing thick, stiff walnut bark used. The product was not a thing of beauty, but it served the purpose: getting someone across a stretch of water.

On the water, the birch-bark canoe sprang to life. Kneeling on its bottom near the stern, the canoeist used different paddle strokes from one side to propel it forwards or backwards and to steer it. No large effort was needed to make it move. Steady strokes pushed it silently and smoothly, hence the canoe's symbolic connection to tranquility and peace of mind.

The bark canoe had no keel and was tippy. It would not tolerate incautious entry or sudden movements, but once underway accepted an experienced paddler as part of its form. It was a well-respected piece of equipment used for fishing, hunting, and gathering wild rice. Indians in southern Canada and some northern states continue to use canoes to gather rice. They paddle into the shallow areas where the rice grows, bend the ripe heads of grain over the canoe, and beat them with a stick or small paddle so the rice falls into the canoe bottom.

If looked after properly, birch-bark canoes could last 5 years with regular use, 20 or 30 if used little. Winter storage was critical. Bark canoes were stored in one of two ways: either kept from excessive light and moisture (elevated upside-down in the shade under a cover) or completely submerged in a lake or pond with rocks as weights.

West Coast native canoe building extended well up into Alaska. This man of the Tlingit tribe was photographed building his canoe in the 1880s in the Cross Sound area of Alaska.

The Skin Canoe

In the Arctic lands of little trees or no trees at all, the bark canoe was an impossibility. The Inuit of the world's northern extremity had to exercise stunning ingenuity to be able to travel on water. And in the Arctic regions, travel on water went beyond a whim: an ability to gather food from the water during the brief season without ice was critical.

The Inuit are known as people of great engineering skills, ingenious in fashioning functional apparatus from scarce supply. The igloo is a marvel of design fitting

The Skin Canoe *by* *John Innes*

environment. So are the parka and leggings—caribou skin worn inside out so the hollow hairs provide more warmth against the body. No less the kayak, found in different forms across the top of the world from Siberia to Greenland.

The kayak was designed for hunting. Usually it was 10 to 25 feet (3 to 7.5 m) long, 15 to 33 inches (38 to 82 cm) across, and shallow at 7 to 15 inches (17 to 38 cm) deep. Low, sleek, and swift, it was used to pursue swimming caribou, polar bears, waterfowl, and sea mammals. It had to be fast, but silent and strong as well—silent to approach sea life, strong to withstand the rough northern seas.

Most designs were so light they could be carried on the head. Most were built to hold one man. Two- and three-man designs existed but were not common. That's probably because the kayak is a union of man and vessel. Once the kayaker is seated in the cockpit, he becomes part of the invention. Only the upper torso is exposed to the outside, the hands and arms an extension of the double-ended paddle that propels the kayak with rocking strokes. The craft's skin covering includes a full apron with drawstring that closes high on the waist to keep water from splashing inside. Alternatively, the kayaker sometimes wears a watertight jacket that fastens to the rim of the cockpit. When the kayak rolls over, as it sometimes does because its narrow bottom is designed to create the least amount of drag across the water, the kayaker rolls with it. Usually a quick, experienced sweep of the paddle will right the kayak. Kayak rolling was sometimes done deliberately to see below the surface or lessen the impact of a big wave; now it is done for sport.

The kayak evolved by region, the construction of each boat carefully undertaken or supervised by the user. Features changed to meet local hunting conditions. Some had more rounded bottoms for speed in chasing swimming caribou. Others had flatter bottoms for more stability in hunting sea mammals in harsher waters.

This watercolor scene by Peter Rindisbacher, painted in the 1820s, shows an Inuit man paddling his kayak through ice-strewn waters. It clearly demonstrates why the kayak was designed for easy maneuverability.

Construction was the opposite of the bark canoe. A sturdy frame was put together and sealskins fitted to it, unlike the bark canoe, where the frame was fitted to the shell. Lack of framing materials was a problem, and much of the pride of construction was in the ability to scavenge material. In many areas wood could be found only by traveling to treeline areas or by gathering driftwood from the ocean shores. Bone was used for some parts. Milled lumber became available only

A voyageur shapes a piece of wood for a bark canoe under construction. He is using an ax, knife, awl, and needle to sew the bark seams together with root strands. This picture originally appeared in the Illustrated London News, March 27, 1858.

after the arrival of the Europeans.

The kayak frame took its strength from wooden gunwales, much heavier than those used in the canoe. Often cut and sculpted from a driftwood log, the gunwales were shaped to have pointed ends, slightly upturned at the bow, sometimes at both ends. The top of the craft was decked except for a manhole. Ribs were made from wood soaked in hot water for softening and shaping. Unlike the bark canoe, the ribs were set in holes drilled into the gunwales. The frame was held together with bone or wood pegs and rawhide lashing. A wood hoop was formed and mounted on the frame to make the manhole.

Natives throughout North America built skin boats, usually stretching animal skins over light wooden frames. The Inuit of the Arctic built large, open umiaks, while far to the south Indians of the Plains made buffalo-skin boats, called bullboats by the fur traders.

Skins for the covering came from seals or caribou. Once cleaned of hair and fat, they were placed in a closed bag, where they became rubbery for easier stretching over the frame. No skin was large enough to cover a frame, so many skins were sewn together. The Inuit achieved waterproof seams by double sewing the skins with sinew and ensuring the stitches did not go completely through any part of the skin. The use of skins made the kayak a high-maintenance item. Skin sheathing sometimes punctured and had to be sealed at sea with ivory plugs. The kayak was out of water at least nine months of the year, and skin sheathing seldom lasted for more than one season.

The Inuit made another skin vessel, the umiak, which was a larger, completely open boat. Most were in the range of 30 feet (9 m) long and 8 feet (2.4 m) wide. They were made of a bone or wooden frame covered with walrus skins and were used to transport families and goods and for whaling expeditions.

Skin boats—sometimes called bullboats—also were used by some Indians in the West and later by explorers and fur traders, but they were not durable. Washington Irving

John B. Wyeth, traveling with fur traders west of the Missouri River to Oregon in 1832, kept notes on the building of a bull boat. He described it as a 12-to-14-foot (3.6 to 4.3 metre) basket of willow ribs covered by buffalo skins. It seemed flimsy but could transport a man, horse, and goods. "At the sight of it, we Yankees all burst out into a loud laugh, whether from surprise, or pleasure, or both, I know not. It certainly was not from ridicule; for we all acknowledged the contrivance would have done credit to old New England."

described one in *The Adventures of Captain Bonneville*, one of his works on the opening of the American West. The boat was launched on the Bighorn River in August 1833 by Nathaniel J. Wyeth, one of Bonneville's group, and was made of three buffalo skins stretched on a light frame, stitched together, and with seams sealed with elk tallow and ashes. It was 18 feet (5.5 m) long and 5½ feet (1.7 m) wide with a round bottom and sharp ends.

"It is surprising what rough shocks and thumps these boats will endure, and what vicissitudes they will live through," wrote Irving. "Their duration, however, is but limited; they require frequently to be hauled out of the water and dried to prevent the hides from becoming water soaked; and they eventually rot and go to pieces."

The use of kayaks and umiaks was common in the North American Arctic until 50 years ago. Until then, Inuit lived relatively isolated from the South, carrying on traditional lifestyles. The opening of the North brought snowmobiles and modern motorized boats that rapidly replaced dogsleds, kayaks, and umiaks, the latter having already begun to fade with the decline in the whaling trade. Traditional kayaks are seldom seen in the Arctic these days, and well-preserved originals are not common even in museums because skin coverings deteriorate.

2

CULTURES JOINED

ON WATER

No single object did more to mix the European and early North American cultures than the canoe. Some might note the importance of the horse brought by the Spaniards, who had the earliest sustained contact with the natives in the south. However, they explored relatively easily on horseback through lands that were mainly desert, semidesert or plains, requiring little help from the natives. Much of their contact with the North Americans was aggressive, their approach one of conquest.

It was different in the heavily forested north. Once ashore on the eastern coast, French and English faced a wall of wilderness. Life was sustainable in coastal colonies, but to penetrate the interior there were only Indian trails and waterways blocked by rapids and falls.

The canoe must have appeared crude, even laughable, when first seen from the deck of a sailing ship capable of

The canoe was the greatest gift of the Indians to the Europeans because it made possible exploration and the fur trade on which North America was built. This 1892 sketch by Frederic Remington from Harper's New Weekly *symbolizes the joining of the two cultures.*

crossing thousands of miles of wild Atlantic water. The chronicler of Jacques Cartier's first voyage to what is now Canada reported one first sighting in 1534:

We caught sight of two fleets of Indian canoes that were crossing from one side [of Bay Chaleur, separating present-day New Brunswick and Quebec] to the other, which numbered in all some forty to fifty canoes. Upon one of the fleets reaching this point, there sprang out and landed a large number of Indians, who set up a great clamour and made frequent signs to us to come ashore, holding up some furs on sticks.

On a second voyage, during which he found the St. Lawrence River, Cartier consulted Indian guides about where this "River to Canada" led. They became serious, telling him that "one could make one's way so far up the river that they had never heard of anyone reaching the head of it." Those who followed after Cartier did reach the head and far beyond, to the Pacific Ocean—and they did it by canoe. Much of the northern portion of the continent was first revealed to Europeans kneeling in bark canoes.

Canoe travel imposed closeness on two different cultures. The Spanish could ride into an Indian village in what is now Kansas, press men into porter service, rape women, steal grain, and ride out to the next adventure. To get anywhere, the French, and to a lesser extent the English, had to climb into a canoe paddled by Indians who knew where to go. They had to portage with them, camp with them, learn how to survive in the wilderness, and adopt some of their clothing, tools, and culture.

Learning the ways of the canoe must have been frustrating, if not downright frightening. No doubt there were hilarious moments when European seafarers used to the solid wood decking of a masted ship tried stepping into a birch-bark canoe with a mind of its own.

"... like everything wild [canoes] are timid and treacherous under the guidance of a white man; and, if he be not an equilibrist, he is sure to get two or three times soused, in his first endeavors at familiar acquaintance with them," wrote George Catlin, the great American painter of Indian life.

Once they learned how to behave in and around canoes, most Europeans found them a marvel of ingenuity. Samuel de Champlain, considered the Father of New France and explorer of much of Ontario and New York, was not impressed by the Indians, whom he said "feed very filthily, and when their hands are greasy they rub them on their hair, or else on the hair of their dogs." However, of their birch-bark canoes he said they were "so light that a man can carry one of them easily."

Champlain also wrote of the canoe:

It is in vain to imagine that any boats could be conveyed past the . . . rapids. But . . . with the canoes of the natives one may travel quickly and through the country as well up the little rivers as up the large ones.

After exploration and settlement, North Americans took to the Indian canoe with a passion. In the latter half of the 19th century the canoe began its transition from transport tool to recreational vehicle. Sir John Glover, governor of Newfoundland, is seen in this photo, circa 1880, with his wife, Lady Elizabeth Glover, and their dog Fogo.

Almost two centuries later, diarist Elizabeth Simcoe, wife of Upper Canada governor John Graves Simcoe, wrote:

To see a Birch Canoe managed with that inexpressible ease and composure which is characteristic of an Indian is the prettiest sight imaginable. A man usually paddles at one end of it and a woman at the other but in smooth water little exertion is wanting and they sit quietly as if to take the air. The canoe appears to move as if by clockwork. I always wish to conduct a Canoe myself when I see them manage it with such dexterity and grace. A European usually looks awkward and in a bustle compared with the Indians' quiet skill in a Canoe.

Catlin also described the beauty of the bark canoe:

The bark canoe of the Chippeways [Ojibwa] is, perhaps, the most beautiful and light model of all the water crafts that were ever invented. They are generally made complete with the rind of one birch tree, and so ingeniously shaped and sewed together, with roots of the tamarack . . . that they are water-tight, and ride upon the water, as light as a cork. They gracefully lean and dodge about under the skillful balance of an Indian.

The birch-bark canoe was described by the young cadet John Henry in Arnold's Quebec expedition as "so light that a person of common strength may carry one of the smaller kind, such as ours were, many hundreds of yards without halting."

Not everyone was totally impressed by the canoe. Malcolm MacDonald, British high commissioner to Canada, wrote in *The Birds of Brewery Creek* in 1947:

Yes, a canoe is an incomparable companion in the Canadian spring and summer and autumn. But in winter it is helpless. When the lakes and rivers freeze life flees from its limbs. Its body grows paralyzed and its spirit dies. Like many animals then, it must hide itself away. Since it cannot migrate like the Swallow, it hibernates like a Bear.

The canoe culture gave the Europeans exactly what they were willing to put into it. Patience, deprivation, and hard work brought rewards of adventure, exploration, new ways of living, and the riches available through furs. Those willing and able to adopt the ways of the new land flourished; those who wouldn't, or couldn't, suffered. One example was Claude-Jean Allouez, who established the famous Sainte Marie among the Hurons mission on Lake Huron in 1665. Father Allouez found the Indian beliefs "false and abominable," despite the fact that Indian offerings to spirits were little different from the offering of the body and blood of Christ at Mass. The Huron didn't like his attitude toward them and responded in kind. They teased him about his poor canoeing skills and made fun of him by suggesting that children carry him on the portages.

He wrote: "The slight esteem in which they held me caused them to steal every article of my wardrobe that they could and I had trouble keeping my hat, the wide rim of which seemed to them well suited against the heat of the sun."

Others more tolerant of the Indian lifestyle took lessons from the Indians on how to travel and survive in the wilderness.

The Nez Percé chief Twisted Hair showed members of the Lewis and Clark expedition how to quickly burn out and hollow large pine trees as dugouts they could use in their quest to find a cross-country route to the Pacific. The Blackfoot also built dugouts from cottonwood trees for fur traders and explorers.

One member of upper European society who embraced canoe travel with a passion was Sir George Simpson, governor of the Hudson's Bay Company from 1821 to 1860. Simpson, called the Little Emperor, had personal Express canoes in which he traveled across the continent many times. Twenty-four to 26 feet (roughly 8 m) long, narrow of beam, these craft were swift, especially when paddled by elite crews of Iroquois. Bows, sterns, and gunwales were painted in bright native designs, and the company flag streamed in the breeze at the bow as Simpson's crew paddled to the skirl of his personal bagpiper.

"It is strange that all my ailments vanish as soon as I seat myself in a canoe," Simpson once wrote. Simpson loved the speed of his special Express canoes and took pride in setting speed records.

Coureurs de Bois and Voyageurs

The coureurs de bois—runners of the woods—developed canoe travel into a culture as they paddled out of the specks

A remarkable record of canoe life in North America is provided by the work of 19th-century artists. Running the Rapids (circa 1881) by Frances Anne Hopkins shows in vivid detail a large birch-bark canoe used by the voyageurs for cross-country exploration and the transport of furs.

of New France along the St. Lawrence and into the heart of central and northern America. They soon became a distinct social class in the new land, a class unknown before in European life. They were neither liked nor accepted by the establishment. They were disrespectful of authority, irreverent, and violent, and when back from the woods they blew their money on alcohol and prostitutes. They were an

offense in the eyes of those trying to establish a colony in a
primitive land.

The coureurs de bois were a product specifically of New
France. After the British takeover of Canada, the men who
paddled for furs became known as voyageurs, a name applied to
canoemen in both the U.S. and Canada. Voyageurs and
mountain men seeking furs opened the U.S. Northwest.

François Paradis in the North *by Clarence Gagnon*

Of the coureurs de bois, New France soldier Baron de La Hontan observed:

You would be amazed if you saw how lewd these Pedlars are when they return; how they Feast and Game, and how prodigal they are, not only in their Cloaths, but upon

Women. Some of them as are married, have the wisdom to retire to their own Houses; but the Batchelors act just as . . . Pirates are wont to do; for they Lavish, Eat, Drink and Play all away as long as the Goods hold out; and when they are gone, they even sell their Embroidery, their Lace and their Cloaths. This done, they are forced to go upon a new Voyage for Subsistence.

Some bad feeling against the coureurs de bois was spawned by envy. They were free spirits who danced only to the rhythms of their own paddle strokes. They lived a wild and dangerous life beyond the stiffness of a colony controlled by the bureaucracies of State and Church.

"We weare Cesars being nobody to contradict us," wrote Pierre-Esprit Radisson, one of the great explorers of North America.

Austere clergymen and civic leaders were alarmed by the growth of coureurs de bois and their canoe culture. The clergy saw the coureurs de bois degrading the Indians with liquor and prostitution, undoing the holiness being expended to save Indian souls. Civic authorities saw a debauchery that hindered efforts to establish European civility in a savage land.

Jean de Lauson, governor of the French colony, tried to stop the growth of the coureurs de bois. He decreed that no one would be allowed to go trading "with the Hurons or other Nations without our previous written consent, under

British royalty was often fascinated by the canoe life of North America. The Prince of Wales canoed the Nipigon River in northern Ontario during a royal tour in 1919.

penalty of a fine." However, neither he nor anyone else could stop the coureurs de bois; the fur trade was too big, too important to Europe. Only money talks when the riches are so phenomenal. Besides, their travels helped New France greatly expand its territory as they ranged in their canoes north of the Great Lakes to Hudson Bay, south to the Gulf of Mexico.

The life of the coureurs de bois and voyageurs in the wilds was the genuine life of North America. It was the life of the Indian who had learned to be a part of nature, taking what he needed to survive, adapting to the environment. The European viewed the wilderness as something to be feared. Animals, fierce weather, the brooding darkness of the woods, the lack of food, the Indians themselves—all were threats to survival. From the fear of the wilderness grew the need to tame it and to control it. The native view was opposite. Woods and waters and animals provided life. Humans were simply part of it, living as best they could, as did the bears and the trees. Everything around them was a gift from a higher being, gifts to be respected and praised, not feared.

Life together in the canoes and along the portages changed both the Indians and the Europeans. They learned from each

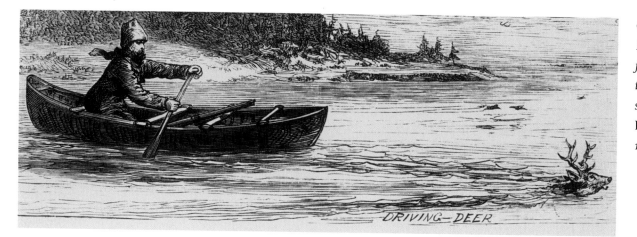

DRIVING-DEER

Originally, the primary use of the North American canoe was in fishing and hunting. This scene of a trapper driving a deer to shore before shooting it appeared in the Illustrated London News *on May 15, 1880.*

other, establishing a culture on which North American society would be built. Some aspects of the building of that society—treatment of the First Peoples, the annihilation of some animal and bird species, and the degradation of the environment—are much regretted today. But the basics of early canoe life in the wilderness—the freedom, the joy of being part of the land, the survival skills—remain a cherished part of North American life.

The Europeans got more than they gave, and what they learned went beyond how to handle a canoe. Their survival initially rested with the Indians. Native herbal medicine was advanced far beyond what they knew. Native agricultural methods were designed to coax vegetables from what was a non-agricultural land. The Indian toboggan, dogsled, moccasin, and snowshoe are examples of Indian inventions the Europeans adopted to build a new life. Native skills were invaluable: how to fish with spear or net; how to find, stalk, and kill game; how to dress it and preserve it to make it last longer; how to tap and boil maple syrup; how to make and maintain life-giving fire; how to quickly build a shelter and a bed that is warm and dry; how to make clothes that could withstand the rigors of nomadic life.

Beyond physical things, the Europeans were exposed to the natives' easier approach to life. Attitudes about living were simple, if perhaps sometimes too fatalistic. Different character traits—patience, acceptance, trust in one's own skills—developed from the harshness of wilderness life. There is no question about its harshness. Aside from the dangers, just the routine of long-distance canoe travel was physically and mentally draining. Trips often lasted four to eight weeks, much longer in explorations. They were up and on the water before dawn and paused only for a midday meal. They paddled and portaged into the evening every day.

Radisson, who wrote in English, described it:

It is a strange thing when victualls are wanting, worke whole nights & dayes, lye downe on the bare ground & not allwayes that hap, the breech in the water, the feare in ye buttocks, to have the belly empty, the wearinesse in the bones, and drowsinesse of ye body by the bad weather that you are to suffer, having nothing to keepe you from such a calamity.

The Europeans eventually applied their boat-building designs to the canoe, producing wood-strip canoes and canoe/boat hybrids that could be rowed. Zola Campbell is seen rowing at Banff, Alberta, during her honeymoon, circa *1910.*

The image of "victualls wanting" seems odd considering the wilds provided fish, birds, deer, moose, bear, and all kinds of vegetable life. But it took time to hunt and gather, and weather often made time short. Corn and dried meat were easy to carry and quick to eat along the trail. The natives taught the Europeans how to dry-smoke thin strips of meat, then roll them in bark for later use. On the trail these could be crushed together with corn and boiled into a soup. In the West, buffalo meat was dried and pounded, then mixed with melted fat and perhaps berries to create a mixture that was put into a buffalo-skin bag. It was called pemmican, from the Cree words *pimmi* (meat) and *kon* (fat).

Much of what the Europeans learned came from women. Coureurs de bois, voyageurs, and other traders often married native women "after the custom of the country," meaning the couple lived as man and wife though not legally married by a clergyman. The marriages were useful to the Europeans. Wives taught their husbands priceless lessons and skills for wilderness living and often were able to persuade members of their tribe to bring in more furs. The joining of the European and North American races created a new people called Métis, who had a significant role in the development of western Canada.

The elite of the colonies looked down upon the coureurs de bois, but they were an important bridge between the European and North American cultures. They also are the

West Coast Indians Returning from the Hunt *by Thomas Mower Martin*

link between today's canoeists and the past. They developed the love for the wilderness, the hunger for freedom, the impatience with organized society, and the skills that remain in today's canoe culture.

3

PADDLING

FOR RICHES

Explorer Jacques Cartier didn't understand what was happening that hot day in 1534 when his ship encountered Mi'kmaq canoeists waving animal skins in Bay Chaleur. The Mi'kmaq wanted to trade, but the French were unable to interpret the waving and were intimidated by this first sighting of natives. Cartier didn't know that the Mi'kmaq had been visited previously by roaming European fishermen who came ashore briefly and traded pots and beads for furs. When the Indians spotted the ship, they saw it as another opportunity to trade.

The Cartier crew didn't trade that day, but they did later in what was the beginning of a fur trade era that lasted 300 years, helped found a continent, and changed the world. All that happened thanks to delicate birch-bark canoes like those paddled by Cartier's Mi'kmaq.

"The great canoes of the Canadian fur trade must be

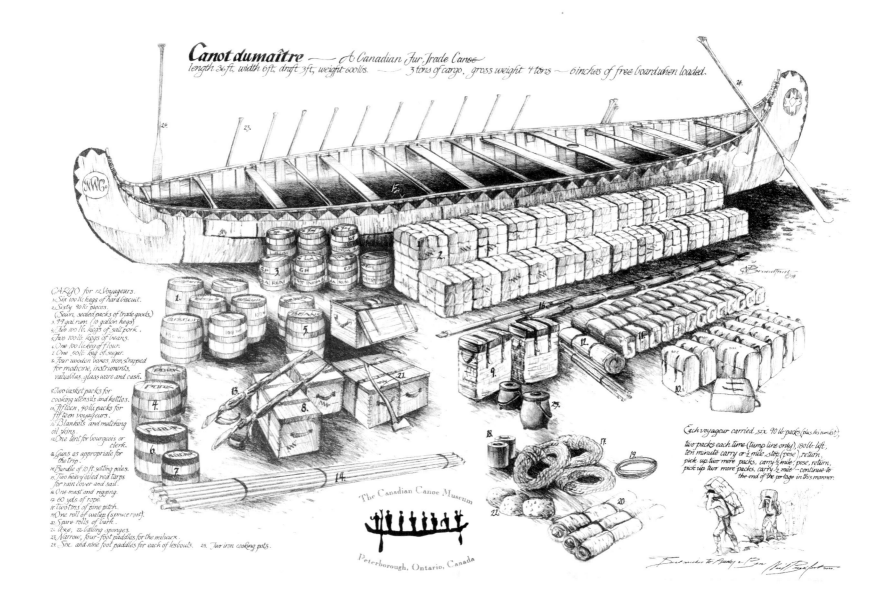

Freighter canoes of the fur trade carried up to 2.3 metric tons of equipment, supplies, trade goods, and furs. This sketch of a Canot du maître *shows the amount of goods that could be packed into one canoe.*

looked upon as the national watercraft type . . . far more representative of . . . national expansion than the wagon, truck, locomotive or steamship," American authors Edwin Adney and Howard Chappelle have written.

Economically, the fur trade pales when compared with world trade in fish, tobacco, grain, and sugar. Historically, though, it rates among the world's most important happenings. The canoe routes of the fur trade were often followed later, during the building of railroads and highways. The trade helped build two countries, the United States and Canada. In the case of the latter, the fur years are considered the defining era in Canada's establishment as a nation.

When Cartier met the Mi'kmaqs, European interest in furs was almost exclusively centered on expensive Russian luxury pelts. That changed about 50 years later when the style for men's and women's hats turned to felt with stiff, broad brims. The North American beaver provided a soft underhair that made the best felt.

The first North Americans attached reverence to the beaver. They believed it could change itself into other animal forms and that it could not be killed without the consent of "the keeper of the game" spirit. It was taken only when needed until human greed fed by the materialism of the fur trade coerced the natives into overhunting it to gain goods.

Beaver were not hard to find. The North American beaver population has been estimated at 10 million before the coming of the Europeans. Colonies of the industrious rodent with the sleek brown fur, sharp buck teeth, and scaly strap-like tail were found in every forest, lake, stream, and pond as far south as Arizona. A canoe ride on most lakes would reveal the chewed stumps of trees taken for lodge and dam building. So strong and sharp were the beaver's teeth that the natives used them as hand chisels. The beaver provided a sizable pelt of long and coarse outer hairs scattered through a fine and dense fur. Adults grow up to 3 feet (0.9 m) long and weigh as much as 66 pounds (30 kg). The meat could be eaten and was considered a delicacy by some.

"The flesh is very good either boiled or roasted but the tail is the best part," adventurer John Long wrote in the late 1800s.

In an odd twist of logic someone persuaded the Roman Catholic Church to allow beaver consumption during Lent, when meat was forbidden. The argument was that the beaver spent most of its time in the water and therefore was more fish than animal.

Once trapped, the beaver were skinned and the pelts scraped clean and stretched on oval hoops for drying and preservation. Bundles of the furs were canoed to a settlement, as the Europeans initially stayed put and waited for the furs to come to them. Demand increased and the furs did not come fast enough. The Indians were reluctant to travel to new territory, so the coureurs de bois obtained their own birch-bark canoes and headed west into the continent's heart in search of a steady supply. When the 17th century ended, they had explored the Great Lakes, the Mississippi River system, and the Great Plains.

The sight of canoes small and large loading and unloading at a village waterfront such as Montreal's was common. In the trading heyday, freighter canoes paddled by 6 to 12 men pushed off in spring from Montreal carrying up to 2.3 metric tons of imported merchandise and business correspondence. These were destined for the head of the Great Lakes, 1,000 miles (1,600 km) away. Out in the wilderness, smaller canoes with crews of five or six set out from posts to deliver furs trapped during the winter. Each freighter canoe carried roughly 30 bales of furs weighing 90 pounds (41 kg) each. The furs were compressed in screw presses and packaged into bales 24 by 21 by 15 inches (61 by 53 by 38 cm). The groups met and exchanged loads at Grand Portage, Minnesota, and Fort William (now Thunder Bay), Ontario, at the head of Lake Superior. The furs went to Montreal and on to England and continental Europe. Trade goods and correspondence were taken on to the outposts and the cycle began again. Later, when the trade moved further west, rendezvous were held annually in the Rocky Mountains of Wyoming and Idaho, where voyageurs, trappers, and traders met to exchange goods and talk.

Life for the canoemen was exhilarating but brutal. Only the strongest could keep up with the rigors of paddling in stormy weather and traversing rough portages carrying canoes, trade goods, and bales of fur. Each man was expected to carry—in fact took pride in carrying—a "pacton" of two 90-pound (41 kg) bales at one time. A Jesuit priest noted it was a rough trade suitable only for those who "are not scared to paddle five or six hundred leagues [roughly 1,500 to 1,800 miles or 2,400 to 2,880 km] in a canoe, live for a year or 18 months on corn and bear fat, and sleep under shelters made of roots and branches."

An army officer who traveled one of the canoe routes in 1798 wrote of the voyageurs:

> No men in the world are more severely worked than are these Canadian voyageurs. I have known them to work in a canoe twenty hours out of twenty-four, and go at that rate during a fortnight or three weeks without a day of rest . . . They smoke almost incessantly, and sing peculiar songs . . . They rest from five to 10 minutes every two hours, when they refill their pipes; it is more common for them to describe distances by so many pipes, than in any other way.

John Jacob Astor, German-American merchant and financier, was reputed to have said that in his fur trade enter-prises he would take one French Canadian voyageur over any three other men.

They soothed their hard life with tobacco smoke, jokes, and smutty songs, which they made up as they paddled. The melodies were rhythmic and helped to keep the paddlers in time. A Scot, John MacTaggart, described their singing in 1829:

> Many of their canoe songs are exquisities particularly the air they give them . . . We must be in a canoe with a dozen hearty paddlers, the lake pure, the weather fine, and the rapids past, before their influence can be particularly felt. Music and song I have revelled in all my life and must own that the chanson des voyageurs has delighted me above all others excepting those of Scotland.

The Route West

Two to three months of this hardship were needed for a return trip from Montreal to Michilimackinac at the strait separating Lakes Michigan and Huron. To get there, they paddled the Ottawa and Mattawa rivers upstream to Lake Nipissing, which they crossed to enter the French River system. The French River took them to Georgian Bay in Lake Huron. En route there were at least 30 to 36 forested portages that included hills, rocks, and swamp. Canoes were

Working a Canoe up
a Rapid *by William
Henry Bartlett*

emptied of cargo and carried varying distances—sometimes
8½ miles (14 km) as in the case of the Grand Portage that led
west of Lake Superior—to the next navigable water. Cargo,
whether it was goods heading west or furs going east, was
strapped to the paddlers' backs, the weight eased somewhat
by tumplines placed across the forehead. Even early on
birch-bark canoes could carry 1,000 pounds (450 kg) of
cargo, and that increased to 3,000 pounds (1,364 kg) when

A classic birch-bark freighter canoe photographed at the Hudson's Bay Company post at Bear Island on Lake Temagami in 1896. The black tree-gum lines illustrate seams where the birch bark was joined or gored for shaping.

larger canoes began to be used early in the 18th century.

Today, anyone can follow the footsteps of the canoemen along the Grand Portage. The U.S. National Parks Service maintains the area as the Grand Portage National Monument. It is open year-round to hikers, backpackers, and

cross-country skiers and can be reached by traveling 36 miles (58 km) north of Grand Marais, Minnesota, or 45 miles (72 km) south of Thunder Bay, Ontario.

The numbers of pelts taken in the interior and paddled out to Montreal were astounding. In the 1620s there were 12,000 to 15,000 pounds (5,455 to 6,818 kg) of beaver pelts arriving each year at the frontier port. This increased to 20,000 (9,091 kg) by 1645, to 89,500 (40,682 kg) between 1675 and 1685, and to 140,000 pounds (63,500 kg) between 1685 and 1687. The supply of beaver and the stamina of the coureurs de bois seemed inexhaustible.

Portaging sometimes was avoided by running rapids, but this could be dangerous. Spills into cold water often meant drowning or cold-induced disease. Many canoemen also died from spills or injuries received in falls while portaging their loads. Dead comrades were buried beside the trail or overlooking a lake, a rough wooden cross marking the spot. Some portages carried clusters of crosses.

The date of this photograph is unknown, but it is certainly from the twilight years of the fur trade. This trapper is smoking the clay pipe favored by voyageurs. The pipe was the sole luxury for the men paddling the fur trade routes.

The weather in the northern forests of North America was seldom kind. Snows came as early as October and late spring snowstorms were possible after ice-out. Rain and humidity around the Great Lakes made travel miserable. Savage blackflies gathered in clouds during the spring and mosquitoes could be unbearable right through the summer. Animals were a threat, particularly in the West where grizzly bears roamed freely and rattlesnakes were common.

Washington Irving in *The Adventures of Captain Bonneville* describes how a grizzly attacked a canoe of voyageurs far west on the Missouri River:

> Just as the canoe was drawing near, he [a swimming bear] turned suddenly round and made for it, with a horrible snarl and a tremendous show of teeth . . . Scarce had they turned the boat when the bear laid his enormous claws on the gunwale and attempted to get on board. The canoe was nearly overturned and a deluge of water came pouring over the gunwale. All was clamour, terror and confusion. Every one bawled out—the bear roared and snarled—one caught up a gun; but water had rendered it useless. Others handled their paddles more effectually and beating old Bruin about the head and claws, obliged him to relinquish his hold.

The miseries were not enough to deter young men from

pursuing their dream of a wilderness life, and that caused problems in the French settlements. New France intendant Duchesneau estimated in 1679 that between 500 and 600 men of the colony were off in the woods at any one time. That wasn't taking into account those "who leave every day." The following year he estimated that 800 of the colony's 9,700 inhabitants were wandering the wilderness in search of furs. Colonist leaders raged that the absence of men was ruining the colony. Women and children were left to fend for themselves and land and cattle were neglected.

The problem did not exist to that extent in New England. The English settlers tended to stay close to home initially, and it wasn't until the fledgling U.S.A. made the Louisiana Purchase from France in 1803 that Americans began the earnest pursuit of beaver and other furs. But in the northern French territory loss of men to the woods was considered so serious that the matter was brought to Louis XIV, who issued a 1681 decree limiting the number of coureurs de bois. Those who ignored it were flogged. Second offenders were branded with the fleur-de-lis, the symbol of France, and third offenders got life on the galley ships. The decree didn't work. Civil authorities continued to decry the coureurs de bois lifestyle and declared it would return the colony to the wild and undisciplined land it used to be.

Finally, Louis got really tough and issued a decree in 1696 restricting fur-trading activities to the establishments

Furs from trapped animals were compressed in a screw press and bundled for easier packing into canoes. Each voyageur was required to portage two 90-pound (40 kg) bales at one time.

along the St. Lawrence River. He ordered that "every person, regardless of rank or condition, [not be allowed] to leave on a trading trip or to go inland for any reason, under pain of the galleys; and requires all Frenchmen settled with or visiting the Natives to take their leave and return, or they will be liable of the same punishment." The freedom days of the original coureurs de bois were over. The fur trade became more organized and the free spirits of the wilderness became laborers for the large trading companies.

Meanwhile, the intense rivalry between France and England had prompted the British to capture the Dutch colonies at New York and establish a northern foothold on the continent through Hudson Bay. By late in the 1600s, the English had formed The Governor and Company of Adventurers of England Trading into Hudson's Bay—the Hudson's Bay Company. It competed immediately with the French fur trade and stretched tensions over the exploration of the New World. Ultimately the tensions led to war that saw the British armies win control of New France in 1763.

The Great Fur Companies

The French had established an efficient system of canoe routes, trading posts, and employees far into the interior. The traders and merchants of Montreal were not about to see this abandoned, despite the British takeover and the Hudson's Bay Company's ambitions. They formed new partnerships with experienced traders from New England. In 1783, a number of these trading groups established the North West Company and pushed far beyond the Great Lakes, across the Plains and into the Rocky Mountains.

The U.S. had now won its independence from Britain, purchased the entire west side of the country from France, and began rapidly moving west in search of furs and an interior route to the Pacific. One of the first into the American fur trade was John Jacob Astor, who, late in the 1700s, began trading furs by buying them in Montreal and shipping them to Europe. In the early 1800s he formed such powerful fur companies as the Pacific Fur Company, the American Fur Company, and the Southwest Company, and established fur forts along the Missouri and Columbia rivers, including the terminus of Astoria in Oregon.

Many others joined in the trade. By 1810, Major Andrew Henry of Pennsylvania had built a fur fort on the Snake River. Two years later the Missouri Fur Company erected Fort Lisa at the mouth of the Platte River. Later still, William Ashley formed the Rocky Mountain Fur Company with such famous mountain men as Jim Bridger, Jedediah Smith, and William Sublette. It was these men traveling by canoe, boat, horseback, and foot who established the routes west for the waves of settlers who followed.

Two Chipewyan Indians show their fur catch at Reindeer Lake, Manitoba, in this 1924 photograph by C. S. MacDonald.

John Jacob Astor, the German immigrant who became the most powerful figure in the fur trade of the American West.

Travel in the Rocky Mountains was treacherous, as is illustrated by one of Astor's expeditions led by Wilson Price Hunt of Trenton, New Jersey. Hunt and his party set out in July 1810 for the Missouri country through the established Great Lakes canoe route. He had taken on supplies and hired voyageurs in Montreal because it was still considered the best place on the continent for equipping a fur trade expedition.

Once west of the Missouri, part of Hunt's expedition tried to descend the Snake River in canoes. It was a disaster. The river became wild and battered the canoes, smashing them and tossing men into the water. One of the most valued voyageurs, French Canadian Antoine Clappine, perished when his canoe carrying five men smashed into a rock. Clappine was able to cling to a rock, but the river flung a smashed canoe at him, sweeping him away.

The competition between the new American companies, the North West Company, and the Hudson's Bay Company was fierce and changed the fur trade. The Canadian companies hired white men and sent them out in brigades to trap the beaver themselves instead of just transporting it. American plainsmen and French Canadian voyageurs blended into a new breed of mountain men who used horses and pack mules more than canoes. They were the same type of men as the coureurs de bois and voyageurs, however, men who hungered for adventure while craving freedom and rejecting authority. They were loud, bold, and aggressive. One group employed by the North West Company attacked and seized Astor's fort at Astoria, an incident that later compelled him to sell it to his northern competition.

The fur trade and the continent it helped to build changed rapidly as the mid-1800s approached. Canada ceded the western lands south of the 49th parallel and the shapes of the two countries were set. Settlement of the West brought wagon roads, ships, and steam trains that pushed the canoe into the role of anachronism along with its native inventors and European converts.

Trapping of furs continues today in a minor way, and some of it is done by canoe. Pockets of natives in Canada and the U.S. trap to help sustain their lives. It is a controversial pastime in the urban world and raises the age-old issue of human welfare versus animal welfare. Whatever the arguments on either side, they should not be allowed to obscure the crucial role of the native peoples in making it possible for the Europeans to build a New World.

4

W A R S   A L O N G
T H E   W A T E R S

T he canoe was not always a symbol of peace
and tranquility. Its history is stained with the
blood of thousands who died in intertribal
wars and, later, in the wars between the
Europeans trying to establish empires in
North America. Many a young man ended life floating face
down in waters mixed with blood and the remains of
shattered canoes. It was the principal vehicle of war in the
North American woodlands until the French and the British
were well enough established to introduce bateaux and lake
ships. Fast, silent, and easily transportable, the canoe was an
excellent craft for the hit-and-run warfare of the times.

In battle, design and construction of the bark canoe
sometimes meant the difference between victory and defeat.
For instance, the Iroquois elm-bark canoe was clunkier than
the Algonquian birch-bark canoe, which was faster and could
turn with the ease of a dried leaf pushed along by a lake

A Cree Indian lands his canoe in a 1910 photograph by Edward S. Curtis.

breeze. Jesuit priests reported witnessing water battles in which the speed and quick handling ability of the birch-bark canoes were the deciding factor in victory. One described a water battle in which 350 French and Ottawas paddling in birch-bark canoes encountered a force of 300 English in fifteen boats.

> The enemy no sooner saw themselves pursued than fear made them drop their arms. It was no longer a contest . . . Whatever be the speed which the increased efforts of row-

ers can give to boats that science and skill of the workmen have made capable of swiftness, it does not approach, by a great deal, the fleetness of a bark canoe; this glides—or rather it flies—over the water with the rapidity of an arrow. Therefore the English were soon overtaken. In the first heat of combat all were massacred without mercy . . .

Few battles over water were planned because of the fragility of the craft. An arrow, a club, a musket ball could quickly cripple a bark canoe, so water battles often were chance encounters. There were some deliberate on-water attacks, however; 350 Indians in canoes attacked a British schooner carrying provisions in September 1763 from Niagara on Lake Erie. The battle was fierce, but the Indians, suffering heavy losses, withdrew. The canoe's most useful purpose was to deliver warriors undetected to a land battle, and then away from it, as quickly as needed.

However, the first amphibious assault in U.S. history was made with birch-bark canoes, when Benedict Arnold attacked Quebec in 1775. Arnold and his men crossed the St. Lawrence River in 40 birch-bark canoes but were beaten back by the well-fortified British.

One of the earliest battles involving canoes that was observed by Europeans occurred in the summer of 1609 at the bottom of New York's Lake Champlain. Samuel de Champlain was traveling in 23 canoes with 2 other Frenchmen and 60 Montagnais and Huron allies, when they encountered

Iroquois. He described the events in his journal:

Evening having come, we embarked in our canoes in order to proceed on our way, and as we were paddling along very quietly, and without making any noise, about 10 o'clock at night on the 29th of the month [July] at the extremity of a cape [Crown Point] which projects into the lake on the west side, we met Iroquois on the war-path. Both they and we began to utter shouts and each got his arms ready. We drew out into the lake and the Iroquois landed and arranged all their canoes near one another. Then they began to fell trees with the poor axes, which they sometimes win in war, or with stone axes; and they barricaded themselves well.

Our Indians all night long also kept their canoes close to one another and tied to poles in order not to get separated, but to fight all together in case of need. We were on the water within bow shot of their barricades.

And when they were armed, and everything in order, they sent two canoes which they had separated from the rest, to learn from their enemies whether they wished to fight, and these replied that they had no other desire, but that for the moment nothing could be seen and that it was necessary to wait for daylight in order to distinguish one another.

A magnificent North West canoe with 12 paddlers and 2 passengers pushes through the choppy waters of Lake Ontario in this 1840 watercolor by Millicent Mary Chaplin.

They said that as soon as the sun should rise, they would
attack us and to this our Indians agreed.

Champlain described a night of shouted threats and insults
between the Iroquois on shore and his people still in their
canoes. When daylight broke, they went ashore for battle.

I saw the enemy come out of their barricade to the number
of 200, in appearance strong, robust men. They came
slowly to meet us with a gravity and calm which I admired;
and at their head were three chiefs . . .

The climax of the confrontation was as swift and bizarre
as the buildup had been dramatic and drawn out. Champlain
lifted his harquebus and downed two of the three chiefs with
one shot. The astonished Iroquois, who had never seen
gunfire, fled.

The disadvantage of paddling to war in a canoe was that
the enemy could predict where you were going. Many
ambushes were set at a "carry," the word of the times for a
portage. Usually there was no choice but to land and risk
attack while hauling goods and canoes over the trail.
Eventually, small forts protected key portages.

Champlain's historic gunshot in 1609 helped the
Iroquois to ripen a hatred for the Huron and the French. In
the early 1640s they captured three Huron canoe flotillas

The Silent Fjord *by*
Belmore Browne

bringing furs to Quebec, then launched other attacks that
over the next few years finished off the Huron. The Iroquois
rampage frightened France's native allies and devastated the
fur trade. Missions were abandoned and the river of furs
became a rivulet. Early in 1653, wrote Jesuit missionary
François-Joseph Le Mercier, New France was on the verge of
bankruptcy:

At no time in the past were the beavers more plentiful in our lakes and rivers and more scarce in the country's stores . . . The war against the Iroquois has exhausted all the sources . . . the Huron flotillas have ceased to come for the trade; the Algonquins are depopulated and the remote Nations have withdrawn even further in fear of the Iroquois. The Montréal store has not purchased a single beaver from the Natives in the past year. At Trois-Rivières, the few Natives that came were employed to defend the place where the enemy is expected. The store in Québec is the image of poverty.

New France could not survive without the furs, so it sent out a garrison commander named Dollard des Ormeaux to turn the ambush game against the Iroquois. In the spring of 1660, Dollard and 16 men set an ambush at the Long Sault Rapids on the Ottawa River and were joined by a few Hurons and some Algonquins. Two canoes of Onondaga arrived and were attacked, but two men escaped. Unfortunately for Dollard they were scouts, and the next day 200 Iroquois warriors paddled into the portage, and the small band of French and allies had to retreat into a dilapidated palisade. The Iroquois laid siege to the palisade, using the French birch-bark canoes as torches to set the palisade afire. The standoff lasted seven days, until the French peered out onto the river and saw it covered with the canoes of 500 Mohawks and Oneidas come to help the

Shooting the Rapids *by Fredrick*
Arthur Verner

Onondagas. Three days later Dollard and his men were overrun.

The sight of so many canoes must have been enough to quiver the bowels of even the most savage fighters. Such shows of canoe force often were done for exactly that reason: to terrify. Sometimes it worked, as in 1673 when Louis Frontenac, governor of New France, appeared in Lake Ontario off Kingston, Ontario, with 120 canoes and 2 flatboats. He planned to display enough military might to frighten the Iroquois on shore. When the Iroquois saw the fleet, they dispatched a single canoe to invite Frontenac to talk peace.

A later governor, Joseph Antoine Lefebvre de La Barre, tried similar tactics in a 1684 campaign against the Iroquois. However, his men were sick with malaria and he was afraid of advancing his battle plan, so he took 200 canoes and 15 bateaux to a meeting with Garangula, an Onondaga chief, at the mouth of the Salmon River on the New York side of Lake Ontario. Garangula was not impressed. He had observed the condition of the French troops and belligerently informed La Barre that he was at the mercy of the Indian forces. The governor knew he was in a spot and immediately concluded a "treaty" that allowed him to steal away the next morning. He returned to Quebec in disgrace and was relieved of his post and recalled to France.

Intimidation was a battle skill well practiced by the natives. Before setting out to war in their canoes, they

This war party heads off to battle in the upper Great Lakes in a model of a decorated bark canoe, circa 1820. The figures in the model are carved.

dressed in colorful battle gear and finery and painted the bare parts of their bodies. Their canoes sometimes were ornamented with the colorful symbols of their totems. Fur trader Alexander Henry, an Englishman born in New Jersey, wrote about the fierceness of war paint after he was captured by Chippewa at Michilimackinac in Michigan:

> They were all in a state of intoxication, and naked, except about the middle. One of them, named Wenniway, I had previously known. He was upward of six feet in height, and had his entire face and body covered with charcoal and grease. Only a white spot, of two inches in diameter, encircled either eye. This man walked up to me. He seized me with one hand by the collar of the coat, while in the other he held a large carving knife as if to plunge it into my breast. His eyes, meanwhile, were fixed steadfastly on mine. At length, after some seconds of the most anxious suspense, he dropped his arm, saying, "I won't kill you!"

Once battle was engaged, body paint mixed generously with blood, and fierceness was no longer a matter of show. People like Henry, the Jesuits, and Champlain described in detail the savagery of wilderness battle. After Champlain shot the two chiefs on the shore of the lake that now bears his name, his Indian allies took an Iroquois prisoner and burned his fingertips and penis with a brand heated in the fire. They tore out his nails, scalped him, and pulled out the sinews of his wrist. Champlain told them to stop, then dispatched the tortured prisoner with a shot to the head. The captors ripped open his body and threw his bowels into the lake near the beached canoes, before chopping his heart into pieces and eating it.

Such encounters became common as fur traders paddled west over the next three centuries. One particularly bloodcurdling incident involved John Colter, a former member of the Lewis and Clark expedition, and trapper John Potts. They were canoeing a branch of the Missouri River called Jefferson Fork in separate canoes when a large group of Blackfoot appeared on each bank. They signaled the canoes to come ashore. Colter did, but Potts refused. The Indians shot an arrow into Potts's leg as he kneeled in the canoe and he fired back, killing one of the tribe. Arrows rained down on the canoe, many of them finding their mark and killing Potts.

What happened next is one of the most famous stories in the exploration of the American West. Colter was stripped naked and set free to run for his life. He ran so hard, he began to bleed from the nose and mouth. The fastest runner behind him was about to launch a spear at him when Colter turned, fought him, and killed him. He ran again, reached a river, and dived in to escape.

Meanwhile, the Blackfoot had pulled Potts's corpse to shore, slaughtered it, and scattered the pieces.

It is difficult to imagine a more sickening contrast in the beauty of the North American wilderness: human entrails in the crystal water lapping against the hulls of birch-bark canoes.

5

TRANSITION

The more things change, the more they stay the same. That aged saying certainly applies in the canoe world. The North American canoe has changed significantly during the hundreds of years of its development. New construction methods have been developed, and manufactured products have replaced natural materials. Yet basic design is little changed since early natives first folded bark to create a long hollow with pointed ends. So are its uses, although degrees of each use have shifted dramatically. Subsistence hunting, fishing, trapping, and gathering, the original primary uses of the canoe, have been diminished by the urbanization of society. Recreation and sport have overtaken them.

The canoe experience has not changed. The canoe is paddled and portaged the same as always; a labor of fulfillment and pleasure even for those who had to use it for getting food, exploring, prospecting, or delivering goods. No other mode of transport, except maybe walking, allows such a close connection with nature.

The only early changes to the canoe were in size. The fur trade demanded bigger canoes capable of carrying more voyageurs and more cargo. Trading records show that in 1700 the trade canoe held three men. By 1725 this had increased to five men, and to seven by 1737. The size kept increasing until the *canot du maître* or Montreal canoe of 36 feet (11 m) and longer became common. Montreal canoes generally ran 32 to 36 feet (10 to 11 m) long and 5 to 5½ feet (1.5 to 1.7 m) wide, and carried 3½ to 4 tons including 7 to 12 paddlers and their gear. Some were built 37 to 40 feet (10.8 to 12 m) to carry 14 to 16 paddlers. The smaller North Canoe was 24 to 28 feet (7.3 to 8.5 m) long and just slightly narrower, carrying roughly 1½ tons and 4 to 6 paddlers. The Indians had altered and improved canoe styles over the centuries, mainly to meet regional needs, and easily adapted to larger canoes that carried heavier loads.

Bark canoes already varied considerably across the continent. The Dene, Athapaskans of the western Subarctic, built a long, narrow canoe partially decked on the ends. It reflected a region that on the north bordered the southern range of the kayak-building Inuit. The same people built a larger canoe modeled after the freighter canoe of the Nor'westers. Each had different uses.

Some Cree canoes were compact and stubby, while

A Kutenai canvas canoe is propped with its paddle beside a lake in Kootenay, Montana in this 1910 photo by Edward S. Curtis.

Eastern Cree built "crooked canoes" with much rocker—the bottom of the canoe the shape of rocking-chair rails. They were designed for carrying heavier loads than canoes with a flatter bottom line.

The Mi'kmaq built an open-water canoe that was hog-sheered—higher in the middle—to give more center freeboard for hauling in fishnets. They also had big river canoes with rounded bottoms, and smaller portage or woods canoes with flat bottoms. Bows and sterns of Mi'kmaq canoes often were more rounded than others, even to the point of being almost circular. In Mi'kmaq canoes the bark always was brought over the gunwales and folded before stitching.

Canoes of the Malecite and other Abenaki tribes had high peaked ends designed to handle both the rivers and tamer coastal waters in the region of Maine, New Brunswick, and Quebec. War canoes were narrower for the speed that was prized by these people. After an attack, the first canoe back home would win a special distinguishing mark. These canoes were highly decorated with paint and porcupine quills, often along the entire canoe sides above the waterline. The decorations sometimes told a story and carried the personal mark—bear totem or fish sign—of the owner.

Algonquian tribes built many hybrids to suit their wide range over Quebec, Ontario, Wisconsin, and Minnesota. End shapes differed from long, round noses to high ends with a "chin" or curl depending on the size of water most often traveled in a particular area. Low, rounded ends created less wind resistance and could be paddled beneath overhanging branches in small streams. An advantage of the high-ended canoes was that they could be overturned on land and used as sleeping shelter.

The Algonquian peoples lived in dense woodlands that required them to portage more than most others. They are believed to have invented the carrying method of using the paddles as shoulder rests. Paddles were lashed across the thwarts so that, when the canoe was turned upside down, the paddle blades came to rest on the shoulders. A loop of hide was strapped on the forehead and tied to a back thwart to prevent the canoe from moving backwards off the shoulders.

The Europeans initially relied on the Indians for canoes, but that changed with the explosive growth of the fur trade. Fur traders needed larger canoes capable of carrying valuable furs and trade goods that must not be lost in the vast waters of the Great Lakes. George Simpson demanded better canoes when he was sent out to North America by the Hudson's Bay Company. He was upset that the North West Company had large, fast freighter canoes specifically designed for the trade. He demanded better birch-bark canoes and got them, including the famous narrow and swift Express canoe that became his trademark.

The fur trade demanded more and more canoes, and canoe factories began appearing as early as 1750 at Trois-Rivières, Quebec. This factory at its peak produced 20 Montreal canoes a year, 36 feet (11 m) by 5½ feet (1.7 m) wide and 33 inches (84 cm) deep. Other factories later operated in areas where birch bark was available, such as Fort William, Ontario. Rolls of bark became a trade item as the demand for canoes grew.

A German cartographer, Johann Kohl, traveling in Wisconsin in 1854 painted a word picture of canoe-building activity: "New canoes are being constantly built around me or old ones repaired and I saw them in every stage of perfection. The Indians expend as many bark canoes as we do hunting boots . . ."

Hokule'a, the Star of Joy, created a renaissance of Hawaiian voyaging culture and history. Hokule'a is a double-hulled sailing canoe built by the Polynesian Voyaging Society and launched on its maiden voyage on May 1, 1975. Since then it has sailed 90,000 miles (144,000 km) throughout Polynesia using wind, stars, moon, and waves as its guiding forces. In February 2000 it arrived home on Molokai after a 9,000-mile (14,400 km) journey from Rapa Nui and is touring the Hawaiian Islands in celebration of its 25 years of voyaging. Hokule'a is called the canoe that has brought the Hawaiian people together through renewed pride in their culture.

The End of the Bark Era

Production of bark canoes became impractical in the 1800s. Bark couldn't stand up in a new era of heavy freight transport and became harder to find. By the late 1800s the Europeans began trying treated canvas instead of bark, then cedar-strip planking. Plank joints had to be caulked and the end product wasn't pretty, yet planked canoes provided an alternative to bark.

Sailcloth had been around for centuries, but nobody seems to have thought about using it for anything beyond making a ship move. Then someone decided to use canvas cloth for patching damaged bark canoes. It could be glued over a crack or hole or along the bark bow seams that were prone to being banged up. The natural progression was to use canvas cloth, sealed and waterproofed, to cover cedar-strip hulls. Thick paper, glued and varnished, was also used for a while.

Canvas and wood-strip canoes were built on molds, returning the Europeans to their preferred method of boat building. Steamed cedar strips were bent around the mold, then attached to the gunwale strips. Planking was nailed lengthwise over the ribs. The canvas cloth was stretched tight, nailed to the gunwales and trimmed. Sizing, then painting and varnishing ensured a watertight product. This canoe was cheaper to build than a straight wood strip

because the planks didn't have to be as tightly fitted and caulking wasn't needed.

Even before the advent of cedar strip and canvas there was a suggestion that metal be used to make canoes. The idea was floated in the early 1830s to David Thompson, considered the best of North America's mapmakers. He was asked to consider building tin canoes for one of his

A large moose-skin canoe built by Slavey Indians at Fort Norman, Northwest Territories. Standing near the bow is F. Ray Ross of the Hudson's Bay Company.

A Salish man paddles a beautiful specimen of a West Coast carved dugout with a long, fine-featured bow. This photo was taken on Vancouver Island circa 1890.

This wood-strip canoe carried bow and stern sails to move it along Lesser Slave Lake in Northern Alberta.

expeditions, but he would have nothing to do with it. Less than 10 years later a sheet-iron canoe big enough to hold 14 paddlers was built for the garrison at Penetanguishene, Ontario, on Georgian Bay. Similar experiments followed and in 1886 a new refining process made aluminum canoe building less difficult. The idea was interesting, but aluminum canoes would not become a presence on the waters until after the Second World War, when aluminum became the material of choice in aircraft. Fiberglass followed, allowing easy molding of any canoe shape at a reasonable price, and now fiberglass and aluminum types are the most common recreational canoes.

By the turn of the 20th century, canvas on thin plank was the standard, highly favored by prospectors, trappers, anglers, and hunters. The best of the wood-canvas canoes

These company logos represent the builders of the finest North American canoes. Old Town Canoe on the Penobscot River in northeast Maine built its first canoe in 1898, although the company was not officially incorporated until 1903. It still operates today.

were built in areas once the domain of the birch-bark builders. The Old Town Canoe Company started on the Penobscot River in northern Maine in 1898 and continues to produce canoes to this day. Peterborough County in southern Ontario was famous for its canoes produced by companies such as Rice Lake Canoe and Peterborough Canoe. The company formed by William and Harry Chestnut in New Brunswick began producing in 1897 the canoe that became known simply as the Chestnut.

Recreation brought the greatest changes in canoe use, design, and construction. Late in the 1800s rail and roads gave easier access to the wilderness areas of central North America. Resort living and cottaging became a lifestyle for the wealthy, and canoeing was a major part of summer leisure living. This led to competitive canoeing and even more design and materials changes.

The Indians had raced canoes for fun and the Europeans took to canoe sports with a passion once the work of turning wilderness to civilized countryside had been accomplished. Regattas began just before 1850 in North America's canoe country and quickly spread. The canoe became known as "the poor man's yacht," and canoe meets were popular by the early 1900s. Many North American towns on water boasted a canoe or boat club. Often these were two-story wood buildings with canoe storage at water level and dancing or other social activities on the second floor.

Canoes and kayaks could be seen on the Thames in England and the Seine in France after 1850, and canoe sports flourished as countries formed national canoe associations. Recreational canoeing was popularized in Europe by English barrister John MacGregor, who designed his own Inuit kayak in 1845 and took it on extended trips across the rivers and lakes of Europe. He wrote books and delivered lectures on his experiences and in 1866 formed the Royal Canoe Club.

In 1924, delegates from national canoe associations met

Whitewater kayaking is a wild and wet sport. Here, Anne Boixel of France runs the Ocoee River in Tennessee during the 1996 Olympic women's kayak slalom competition.

in Copenhagen and established the Internationella Representantskapet for Kamotidott (IRK) to set rules for canoe racing. That same year canoe/kayak racing was introduced to the Olympics as an exhibition sport. The IRK argued for recognition as a full medal sport, but the International Olympic Committee (IOC) refused. The IRK became the International Canoe Federation in 1946. The IOC finally consented and canoe/kayak became a medal sport at Berlin in 1936. Nineteen nations competed in eight sprint events: single and pairs kayaks of 1,000 and 10,000 m, single and pairs folding canoes, and single and pairs Canadian canoes. Women's competitions were added in 1948 and whitewater slalom canoe/kayak appeared in 1972 and was added in 1992. Sprint and slalom were run in September 2000 at the Sydney Olympics.

Sprint competitions are held on flat water with competitors assigned to lanes. Women race in kayaks only, while men race in kayaks and canoes. The men's and women's slalom competitors must negotiate 20 to 25 gates in turbulent water over a 300 m (1,000 ft.) course.

6

THE POWER OF

SYMBOLISM

T*he Spirit of Haida Gwaii* paddles silently in Washington, going nowhere but linked spiritually to its mother form also paddling through time hundreds of miles north in Ottawa. Its fantastic passengers, animal, human, and a mixture of both, bite and claw each other in close quarters as they paddle beyond the rim of the world.

What is *Haida Gwaii*? Where is it going? A lifeboat carrying the remnants of a forgotten people? Perhaps a diplomatic mission to another country? Or is it just a vessel lost in a dream, moving on, as its sculptor once said, but forever anchored in the same place? Maybe it is simply a canoe of "beings looking for other beings to speak to, feast with, trade with, perhaps to intermarry with, not for a place to plant a flag," as Robert Bringhurst wrote in *The Black Canoe: Bill Reid and the Spirit of Haida Gwaii.*

Whatever it is, there is powerful symbolism in the fact

Bill Reid's The Spirit of the Haida Gwaii *at the Canadian Embassy in Washington.*

that this five-tonne black bronze sculpture and its white plaster cast reside in the capitals of the two countries whose borders and cultures were shaped by the canoe. The vision of the late Bill Reid, *Haida Gwaii* is a symbolic bridge between cultures. It is also a statement about all living creatures journeying together through life. Reid, considered one of Canada's most important artists, sculpted the work for a new Canadian embassy in Washington. A massive piece almost 20 feet (6 m) long and 13 feet (4 m) high, it was installed by crane in 1991 while its plaster cast was placed in the Canadian Museum of Civilization in Ottawa. A close facsimile is displayed at the international airport in Vancouver, B.C.

The Spirit of Haida Gwaii symbolizes the relationship between the canoe and the human journey; a journey that many tribes believed started with birth and continues after death. Some believe that when a person dies, he or she is

Paddles used with West Coast dugouts have become pieces of art.

carried to the Land of the Dead in a spirit canoe. The Slave and Chipewyan people believe that at death the soul takes a long journey across a lake in a stone canoe. If the person has lived a good life, the canoe travels safely to an enchanted island where there is bountiful game and firewood. If the person has lived an evil life, the canoe sinks and the soul spends eternity in the cold depths. Stories of canoes ferrying people between worlds are seen in rock paintings found at many sites along the great canoe paths of North America.

Canoes sometimes served as sepulchers or were left at a burial site for the spirit's journey. About 150 years ago the remains of an aboriginal child were found in a burial cave in Newfoundland. In the tomb were toys and a 3-foot (1 m) bark canoe, crafted carefully as if it were to be paddled on a nearby lake or stream. The fine detail of the canoe's construction showed the importance the child's tribe placed on the final canoe journey.

The Canoe and the North American Psyche

Today, even with the transition to a mainly urban society, North American culture brims with connections between the canoe and the human experience. Canoes are in our art, music, writings, and films. Canoes float in and out of fashions. It is the North American symbol of serenity, independence, and romance. Many a love song and movie scene celebrates young love paddling quietly through tranquil waters.

One of Hollywood's most famous canoe scenes has Nelson Eddy, dressed in the scarlet of the Royal Canadian Mounted Police, crooning to Jeanette MacDonald as he paddles her through the wilderness in the 1936 movie *Rose Marie*. Hollywood also used the canoe to promote Marilyn Monroe with a photograph of her trying out a canoe during a break in filming *River of No Return* in 1954.

Moonlight and love are common elements in North American songs about canoeing.

"O, come with me in my light canoe . . . O, come with me and be my love," urges the old tune "Light Canoe," published by Auner and Johnson of Philadelphia.

"Dreams, dreams, do you remember, Love," asks the

The connection between canoes and romance developed late in the 19th century and continues to this day. This couple was photographed in 1908.

1916 song "On Lake Champlain." "On Lake Champlain in our little birch canoe?"

Similarly, "A Little Birch Canoe and You" from 1918 and "Beautiful Ohio" of the same year extol the wonder of canoes, moonlight, and love.

Canadian author and historian Pierre Berton was somewhat more descriptive about canoes and love when he said in 1973: "A Canadian is somebody who knows how to make love in a canoe."

Lovesick lumberjacks climb into a flying canoe to visit their girlfriends on New Year's Eve in the famous French Canadian folk tale "La Chasse-galerie" (The Flying Canoe). On its return, the flying bark canoe strikes a treetop and

A painting by Octave Henri Julien of the French Canadian folk legend La Chasse-galerie

spills its tipsy paddlers into the snow for a lesson in drunken canoeing.

But the canoe song with the most enduring message was the "Paddle Your Own Canoe" waltz composed by W. S. Milton and published by Carncross and Company of Philadelphia in 1870. The tune and most of the words are long forgotten, but the title remains a statement about doing your own thing.

> Never give up, when trials come,
> Never grow sad and blue,
> Never sit down, with a tear or a frown,
> But paddle your own canoe.

George Catlin's 1846 painting Deer Hunting by Torchlight in Bark Canoes

Canoes have appeared on our postage stamps and currencies. The Fairfield County Bank in Connecticut issued a one-dollar bill around 1840 showing an Indian paddling a canoe with a bow in the shape of an animal head. In 1996 a 90-cent commemorative stamp carried Bill Reid's *Spirit of Haida Gwaii* as the latest in a long line of Canadian stamps showing canoes.

Early artists left an impressive legacy of art illustrating the canoes and wilderness culture that helped build North American society. The works of George Catlin, frontier painter Paul Kane, Frances Ann Hopkins, and Seth Eastman, U.S. Army officer and painter, are priceless records of native life and the exploration and settlement of the continent.

Catlin paintings such as *Canoe Race Near Sault Ste. Marie, Michigan* (1836–37) and *Deer Hunting by Torchlight in*

Frances Ann Hopkins'
painting Canoes in a
Fog, Lake Superior,
1869

Bark Canoes (1846–48) record not only the features and
activities of the Indians but the types of canoes used.

Hopkins was the wife of George Simpson's secretary. She
traveled regularly with Simpson's entourage and her
paintings of the fur trade canoes and the people who
paddled them are considered North American treasures. The
quality of her work is almost photographic. Her *Bivouac of a
Canoe Party* is so detailed it shows two different types of
paddles used on Montreal canoes.

The Group of Seven, formed in the early 1900s, often

Arthur Lismer and Tom Thomson on Canoe Lake in Algonquin Park, 1914.

traveled by canoe on painting expeditions into the north woods. One of its most famous members, Tom Thomson, drowned while canoeing alone on Canoe Lake in Ontario's Algonquin Park. The members made many sketching trips into the Great Lakes woodlands, where they discovered the distinct light of the northern landscape. One of their followers, Emily Carr of Vancouver Island, painted *War Canoes: Alert Bay* in 1912, which sold in the spring of 2000 for $1 million.

A toy canoe set free to see the world has taught hundreds of thousands of children about life around the Great Lakes. *Paddle-to-the-Sea*, the U.S. children's classic written by Holling C. Holling in 1941, is still found in libraries and sold in bookstores. The 1966 film version by the National Film Board of Canada was photographed and directed by Bill Mason of Ottawa, considered a guru of modern canoeing.

In *Paddle-to-the-Sea*, a native boy living in the woods near Lake Nipigon north of Lake Superior dreams of canoeing across the Great Lakes and down to the Atlantic. He knows he can't, so he carves a miniature canoe in which sits an Indian and the supplies he needs to take him on the long journey. Paddle rides the melting snows into a brook, on to the Nipigon River, and into Lake Superior. During his four-year journey Paddle has many adventures and witnesses life along the Great Lakes. The film, which won 10 awards including an Oscar nomination, is brilliantly photographed

The canoe as a poetic symbol first entered America's heart through the writings of its most beloved early poet, Henry Wadsworth Longfellow. Before Longfellow's time Americans had little culture of their own, being too busy shaping a new country from wilderness. Longfellow wrote about a developing America, its people, landscape, and history. His Song of Hiawatha *caught the American imagination and was a favorite for generations of children. The story of Hiawatha introduced average people not only to the native Americans' canoe but to their customs and language.* Chee-maun, *Hiawatha's birch canoe (from the Ojibwa word* jiimaan, *canoe), and* Gitchi Gaamee *(Great Lake) remain well recognized today throughout North America.*

and gives vivid impressions of the landscape and wildlife around the lakes. Despite being 60 years old, *Paddle-to-the-Sea* continues to have an incredible following. The book has a five-star reader rating at Amazon.com and is often on back order.

Mason, who died in his log home outside Ottawa in 1988, is an icon in canoeing. His books, including *Path of the Paddle* and *Song of the Paddle*, have instructed people around the globe how to canoe and travel in the wilderness.

Another icon, and one who helped bring canoe culture to urban society, is Omer Stringer, guide and teacher, who was raised in Algonquin Park, which was set aside in 1893 as an Ontario preserve of 3,000 square miles (78,000 hectares) and 2,000 charted lakes. In the 1980s his name was on the front of every Beaver Canoe shirt produced by Roots shoes and clothing company—"Beaver Canoe. Built by Omer Stringer." Stringer was the son of a park ranger and grew up paddling. He worked as a canoe instructor for a variety of groups including the YMCA and Boy Scouts. He was a major influence on modern canoeing techniques and outdoor travel.

Stringer and Detroit prizefighter Lou Handler founded Camp Tamakwa in Algonquin Park in 1936. It still operates as a summer camp. It was at Tamakwa that Stringer met Michael Budman and Don Green, two young lads from Detroit who became camp counselors. They later founded the Roots shoe company, and when they planned to start a new wood-canvas canoe company, they picked Stringer to be in charge. The canoe operation was not well established when Stringer died in 1988, but the Beaver Canoe logo made him famous. Stringer also was featured in an instructional film called *Paddle and Portage* and in 1975 produced *The Canoeist's Manual*, a pocket guide to canoeing.

In terms of preserving canoe history, the most important modern-day icon is Edwin Tappan Adney (1868–1950), artist and writer (*The Klondike Stampede*). Adney was born in the U.S. and later lived in New Brunswick, and is credited with saving the art of birch-bark canoe construction from oblivion. He constructed more than 100 one-fifth scale models of different types of canoes, which are now housed at the Mariners' Museum in Newport News, Virginia. His work in collaboration with Howard Chappelle is collected in *Bark Canoes and Skin Boats of America*, which is considered the most authoritative book on the North American canoe.

Adding to the work of Adney has been Kirk Wipper, a University of Toronto professor who between 1957 and 1990 collected more than 600 canoes. He had a summer camp in Haliburton County, Ontario, called Camp Kandalore and began collecting canoes as a hobby. He organized the collection into a museum and in 1995 turned it all over to a group that established the Canadian Canoe Museum in Peterborough, Ontario.

The canoe's most powerful symbolism, in terms of

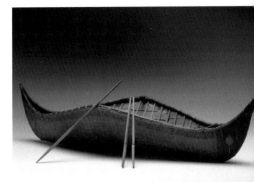

A model of a Beothuk canoe as reconstructed by Edwin Tappan Adney. Adney used the descriptions of explorers, traders and an unusual burial site find of toy canoes to recreate this Beothuk model. This unusual canoe was turned upside down and used as a shelter by the Beothuk. The shorter pieces of wood near the model were used as tent poles.

enduring daily impact, is its link with the environment. It is a symbol of clean water, of carrying only what you need, and of treading carefully in nature's delicate spaces. In the beginning, the birch-bark canoe was made of natural materials and returned to nature when man was finished with it—the perfect environmental product. Today, the environmental impact of its manufacture and use are much more significant, but the canoe, whether wood, aluminum, or plastic, is a symbolic reminder of our stewardship of the land.

The Man Called Grey Owl

The canoe and the beaver were pushed onto center stage as environmental symbols in the late 1920s and early 1930s when a man called Grey Owl paddled his way into the environmental conscience of the English-speaking Western world. The *Atlantic Monthly*, in a January 1990 article, wrote that some people believe Grey Owl should rank with John Muir and Rachel Carson in the environmentalists' pantheon.

Grey Owl lived among the Ojibwa in the Temagami region of northeastern Ontario, trapping and living off the land. Pressed by his Iroquois companion, he began to develop a conscience about killing animals. One day he rescued two beaver kittens, whose mother he had killed, and

Grey Owl paddling his canoe on Lake Ajawaan, Saskatchewan, in 1933 or 1934. His writings and lectures on saving the beaver helped to create a new environmental consciousness.

that relationship brought about the end of his trapping days and put him on the road to becoming an environmentalist.

Late in the 1920s he started a beaver colony and wrote magazine articles on saving the beaver. He lectured at a resort in Quebec and by 1930 attracted the attention of National Parks of Canada, which made a film of his work with beaver. The parks department decided to support Grey Owl and the beaver in Riding Mountain National Park in Manitoba, then in Prince Albert National Park in Saskatchewan. His fame grew as he wrote books. He toured England in 1935 and 1937 and gave a command performance for the king and his two daughters, one of whom is now Queen Elizabeth, and who is reported to have jumped up at the end of the lecture to exclaim: "Oh, do go on!"

Grey Owl died in 1938 at age 49. The newspapers immediately reported that he was a fraud. Grey Owl was Archie Belaney, born in Hastings, England, and raised by his aunts. He had been a child obsessed with all things Indian and struck out for Canada when he was 18. More revelations showed him to be a bigamist and binge drinker, a man carrying the emotional scars of abandonment by his ne'er-do-well father. His Indian persona was a fraud, but the image of Grey Owl quietly canoeing across a beaver pond remains a statement about the need for a balance between civilization and nature. The 1999 Richard Attenborough film *Grey Owl* renewed interest in his life and work. His books are still read, and to many in the conservation movement he is a mentor.

The environment, the human journey, a way of life, the bonds between two sister countries, part of a nation's soul: the canoe is a symbol of all these. Its most important symbolism, however, remains the property of the people who invented it. The canoe travels in the spirituality of the tribes who used it. For some, it is a symbol of hope in the revival and preservation of their culture. Along the Pacific Northwest Coast, new canoes are being carved and paddled as the aboriginal peoples seek to restore pride in their history and culture. In 1984, as part of the State of Washington centennial celebrations, tribes in western Washington carved cedar canoes and took them on journeys to Suquamish and Seattle. Other canoe projects and voyages followed. Bill Reid carved *LooTaas* for paddling to Expo '86 in Vancouver. In July 1993 tribes from as far south as Suquamish, Washington, paddled hundreds of miles north to visit tribes in Bella Bella, British Columbia.

On the West Coast of Vancouver Island, the Ocean Going Canoe Society organizes canoe journeys along the Northwest Coast. One fleet of five canoes took a two-day journey in 1998 from the T'Sou-ke Reserve across the international border to Neah Bay, Washington. One of the young participants wrote later that the power of the journey was the connection to the environment and to her ancestors.

Such trips do more than revive the history of the canoe culture. When a canoe is carved and paddled, other cultural artifacts and practices are given new life. Paddles, tools, and traditional clothing must be made. Singing, dancing, welcoming, and gift ceremonies are all renewed. The canoe revival is seen not only as a symbol of hope, but as a way of healing the hurts of the past. In parts of the Northwest the people now take pride in calling themselves the People of the Canoe Nations.

7

THE POWER
OF THE JOURNEY

Each outing in a canoe is a journey of self-discovery. What person paddling across reflections in morning waters does not see the inner self? The serenity of canoeing strips us of all but the essentials and encourages us to consider our place in the universe. Mind clutter drains away, like water dripping from a paddle blade, and makes space for clarity of thought.

Most of our canoe trips involve personal discoveries that are small and simply refreshing. Some are powerful and healing. A few are deliberate journeys of reorientation that can be life-altering, such as that of Ann Linnea, a Minnesotan who in 1992 circumscribed Lake Superior in a kayak to find her spirituality after the death of her best friend. The canoe is a spiritual vessel that transports us into a more basic way of life, a more basic way of thinking.

Eric Sevareid, the renowned television commentator,

started his adult life with a 2,250-mile (3,600 km) canoe adventure. At 17 he and 19-year-old friend Walt Port paddled from Minneapolis to York Factory on Hudson Bay in an incredible coming-of-age adventure that Sevareid documented in *Canoeing with the Cree.* It was a punishing trip and it would have been simple just to give it up, but Sevareid recalled later: "I knew instinctively that if I gave up now, no matter what the justification, it would become easier forever afterwards to justify compromise with any achievement."

Pierre Elliott Trudeau, former Canadian prime minister, tried to explain in his *Memoirs* why people feel the urge to canoe off into the wilderness.

> I think a lot of people want to go back to the basics sometimes, to find their bearings. For me a good way to do that is to get into nature by canoe—to take myself as far away as possible from everyday life, from its complications and from the artificial wants created by civilization. Canoeing forces you to make a distinction between your needs and your wants.

One example of a powerful journey is found in the diary of Howard Holtman of Winnipeg, Manitoba, who in July 1995 canoed Ontario's Woodland Caribou Park alone for 32 days as a way of celebrating his 50 years of life. His

Once exclusively the pastime of men, wilderness canoeing has become a family recreation.

descriptions of the land are rich and his thoughts are those of a man who has accepted himself as a part of nature. A couple of excerpts:

DAY 6, JULY 12

A short distance ahead I came upon some old Indian pictographs and took a bunch of pictures. The rock paintings depicted a buffalo, a canoe, a man, a wolf, and some other objects. I couldn't help but think about that other paddler who many years ago stopped at this same spot and drew these. I bet the surrounding area looked exactly the same then as it does now.

Day 29, August 4

[Holtman approaches a peninsula on Haggart Lake where there is a small rock cairn built in memory of his son Michael, who died at age 16 in 1989.]

Today I travelled from Haven Lake, through Adventure Lake, Bulging Lake and down into Haggart Lake, past Michael's cairn. As I approached, I could feel my chest tighten and pulse quicken as the flood of memories of my precious son poured forth. I stopped, sat by the cairn, looked out over the still water, and for a long time, just thought about all the things we had done together, what a great little guy he was, and how much he would have loved this trip. I miss him incredibly. Every day I feel his presence, but never so much as when I'm out in the wilderness. He's like a soft breeze always around me, always refreshing, always comforting, always encouraging. After some time, I continued on my way, with a soft breeze over my shoulder, gently helping me along.

Canoeing is not always about being alone. It is also about sharing wilderness experiences and forming networks and lifetime friendships. One of the first canoe friendship networks was established in 1951 during a diplomatic dinner

The beaver, so sought-after by the fur traders, is still relatively plentiful throughout North America. Their dams along canoe routes sometimes make the water better for paddling, but they can create a bit of portage work as well.

party in Ottawa. The outdoors types at the party, including Eric Morse, the national director of the Association of Canadian Clubs, kidded the foreign diplomats about not being able to truly understand Canada until they had canoed its wilderness. The diplomats took up the suggestion.

This dinner talk was the start of The Voyageurs, the first major recreational canoe network in North America, and it brought together two of the continent's most important wilderness canoeists of the 20th century, Morse and Minnesota conservationist and writer Sigurd F. Olson.

The Voyageurs headed west in 1952 to Quetico Park along the Ontario–Minnesota border and in 1954 were joined by Olson. They paddled the old Grand Portage fur trade route, becoming one of the few groups (if not the only one) since the fur trade days to canoe the Grand Portage–Fort Frances,

Ontario, route in its entirety. The Voyageurs made 11 major trips between 1951 and 1964, including the Churchill River in Saskatchewan, the Camsell and Great Bear rivers in the Northwest Territories, and the Pukatawagan to Thompson, Manitoba. Olson wrote *The Lonely Land* from the Churchill trip and Morse wrote *Fur Trade Routes of Canada/Then and Now*.

The Voyageur trips helped Olson gather material for another eight books, including *The Singing Wilderness*, that created a new genre of nature writing and won him in 1974 the John Burroughs Medal, the highest honor for writers about nature. Olson taught for most of his life in Ely, Minnesota, until he became a full-time writer and professional conservationist in 1947.

Both Olson and Morse ignited a passion for wilderness canoeing. Networks of canoe trippers grew out of their friendships and writings, and from the reports of The Voyageurs' adventures. Craig Oliver, Ottawa bureau chief of the CTV television network, says his friend Morse was the bridge between the canoe's role as a working tool and its emergence as a recreational vehicle. "Eric was the guru, the rabbi, the center of the network. He is considered the great guru by many canoeists who had never even met him," reminisces Oliver.

Morse persuaded the Hudson's Bay Company to start a program called U-Paddle in which wilderness canoeists could rent canoes at one HBC outpost and drop them at another. The program, which operated between 1963 and 1984, opened the Arctic to wilderness canoeists in Canada, the U.S., and Europe because it got around the fact that it was simply too expensive to ship canoes into the North. Another important achievement was providing a third dimension for maps used in wilderness canoeing. Previously, maps simply indicated rapids, but that could range from a strong current to a waterfall. Morse's notes of rivers provided detail on the severity of rapids, making rivers much safer for recreational canoeing.

While Morse offered practical assistance to modern-day canoeists, Olson provided wilderness spirituality. "He made wilderness and life sing," said George Marshall, a former president of both the Sierra Club and the Wilderness Society.

Canoe networks like the ones encouraged by the work of Olson and Morse now exist throughout the world. One such—a group of young people called the French Club— provides an example of how friendships forged along a canoe route are retained over the years. Marcella Austenfeld, who lives in Oakland, California, recalls being invited in 1995 to join the French Group on a trip into Quetico Provincial Park, part of Olson's old canoeing grounds in the Ontario– Minnesota boundary waters. The group of young people was missing one paddler and she was invited as an alternate. "At the time I would have never thought that my role as a

In the late 1800s a man called Nessmuk paddled the Adirondacks, breaking a trail for future generations of minimalist campers. He carried only 26 pounds (11.8 kg) of gear, including a cedar-strip canoe reputed to weigh 10 pounds (4.5 kg). It was built by the legendary canoe maker J. Henry Rushton. Nessmuk was the pen name of George Washington Sears, who wrote for Forest and Stream *magazine in the early 1880s. His written works* Canoeing the Adirondacks with Nessmuk: The Adirondack Letters *of* George Washington Sears *and* Woodcraft and Camping *are still popular today.*

substitute would lead to the creation of lasting friendships," she says.

The lives of the French Group members have changed over the years. There have been marriages, moves, children, and fewer trips, but the bond created during their canoe adventures. Élise Parent of Toronto, one of the organizers of the French Group, explains why:

> The feeling of accomplishment when you get to the end of a portage is great. At the end of the day, you are tired and your muscles hurt. You sit with your friends around the fire and listen to the cry of the loons. It is magic. You feel very close to your friends because you have shared the experience, which can be intense at times. Yes, everyone moves on eventually, but I think you stay close because you have seen a side of people you don't often have a chance to see in your daily life.

Canoe journeys almost always provide lessons about the power of nature and the frailty of humans against its forces. Howard Holtman describes being caught in a series of thunderstorms during his 1995 trip.

DAY 21, JULY 27

At about 12:30 the second storm hit. Fork lightning all around me . . . so close there were spots before my eyes after it flashed and my fingers tingled. The thunder was so loud my ears hurt. White caps formed on large waves all across the lake. Expecting each moment to be my last, I made a dash (ha!) for shore and finally made it to a small island that had enough space for a tent. The wind was so strong paddling was impossible and I was grounded, so around 2:30 p.m. I started to put up my tent for the night. With the tent laid out on the ground, but not up, the third storm hit. A combination of the first two—heavy rain, lightning and thunder, plus hail (not large, about quarter inch in diameter). The tent was soaked with about an inch of water all over the floor inside. I managed to get the tent up, wiped it out and crawled inside for a nap while it rained some more. The rain stopped around 7 o'clock. I made a fire, which took a bit of work after all the rain, had dinner, and decided to call it a day. Actually, I called this day many things, but they're not fit to print.

Jim Hegyi of New Berlin, Wisconsin, paddled in 1996 through an area of the Ontario–Minnesota boundary waters destroyed by a forest fire the previous year.

One of the thrills of wilderness canoeing is encountering the unusual, such as an unexpected snowfall or the devastation of a forest fire.

The Florida Everglades, at one time penetrated only by Seminole dugouts, now provide a very different paddling adventure for recreational canoeists.

The northern shore comes into view, and we suddenly realize how devastating the Bird Lake fire was. There is a feeling you get when winter is coming; an empty feeling as the green goes out of the land, and you know that for a long time, the earth will be barren and cold. As we came close to the burned shore, this feeling crept into our canoe; we did not speak. Slowly and quietly, I steer the canoe along the shoreline of one of the islands near the park entry point. I expected black to color the land, but it is white rock that now dominates. Many trees are burned only slightly, but dead nonetheless, for the soil is all gone.

We pass another group of two canoes fishing near the channel leading into Bitchu Lake and paddle slowly into a haunting landscape. The shores, normally a lush green, are now bare. Stark white rock covers the land, as though the earth itself had died and left only its bones to bleach in the sun. Most trees are still standing, and some have patches of green on their branches, but a telltale black mark at the base of each trunk marks them for death by starvation. We again fall silent as we drift through the channel.

Every canoe route has its ghosts. In Algonquin Park it is the mysterious death of Group of Seven artist Tom Thomson who, although he drowned before the Group was named, is considered a part of it. The Nahanni River of the Northwest Territories has its legend of Deadman Valley. Gold seekers tried using the Nahanni as a route to the Yukon gold fields during the rush of the 1890s. Some were never seen again. Two prospectors, Charlie and Willie McLeod, were found in 1906 headless and tied to trees.

Further east in the Northwest Territories, canoeists can stop at the Thelon River cabin where three men starved to death. The group was led by John Hornby, a mad Englishman with a reputation for not thinking ahead and allowing himself to be guided by whims. In 1926 his whim was to cross the

Arctic Barrens to the Thelon forest and live off the land. The three would build a cabin, pack the larder with caribou and fish, and spend the winter trapping.

Hornby, about 50 at the time, missed the caribou migration, and by late November the men had no meat and were eating frozen fish. By Christmas they resorted to eating wolverine. By April they were eating bones and wolverine skins, which bound their bowels so badly they had to use tubing and a glass test tube to give each other soap and water enemas. Hornby died in agony on April 16, three days after Edgar Christian, an 18-year-old tenderfoot, wrote in his diary that Harold Adlard, a 27-year-old handyman, had become "absolutely unhinged and crazy." Adlard died on May 4. Christian wrapped him in a blanket and placed him outside the cabin door beside Hornby, who was wrapped in burlap.

Spring was late that year and the snowstorms blew into May. Christian kept a clear head and documented his own slow and painful death. On June 1 he wrote that he was weak and his heart was giving out. His diary ended there. He placed it inside the cabin stove and left a note that read: WHO LOOK IN STOVE.

Rolf and Debra Kraiker of central Ontario took their two sons, then 8 and 5, down the Thelon in 1994, with friend Herb Mayr and his 13-year-old son, Mat. Rolf described in his journal the visit to the Hornby cabin:

Grave markers of the three members of the Hornby expedition along the Thelon River in the Northwest Territories. The markers are a reminder to all wilderness canoeists of the consequences of poor planning and preparation.

We made camp at a fairly good site just below John Hornby's cabin. The cabin isn't quite where it appears on the map, but a little farther upstream. We noticed the location because of the obvious tree stumps, which look very out of place here . . . The mood at the campsite is somber. While we eat supper, I read excerpts from the diary of Edgar Christian to the kids. They listen to the story of starvation . . . The kids listen intently and ask questions at the end of the passages.

The next day they visited the cabin site.

Herb, Deb, Brendan and I take a walk to Hornby's cabin before breakfast. The three humble graves with their plain

Amid the hustle-and-bustle of our 21st century world, what could be more appealing than an early morning mist and the quiet sound of a paddle as it slices through the water.

wooden cross markers in this lonely land cause us all to reflect. We look at the cabin, see the caribou remains, walk in the forest to see where they cut lumber and imagine the three of them slowly starving to death with no hope of rescue. Brendan asks a million questions as he and I move around to document the site. He asks about "the boy" (Edgar Christian), what he was doing here, where he came from, what his parents were thinking. He obviously absorbed a lot of the conversation at the supper table last night.

The early canoe explorers of North America kept journals and diaries as a necessary part of their work. This practice of writing beside the campfire or pausing on the lake to jot an observation or a thought has become a tradition, and we are all the better for it. Libraries are filled with hundreds of canoeing books and magazine articles containing real-life accounts of wilderness paddling. This treasury of stories expands every day now through the Internet, where canoeists and kayakers find satisfaction in publishing stories of their own trips.

8

CANOEING IN THE
21ST CENTURY

A few years ago Koji Ishikura of Tokyo received an unusual graduation gift. His parents gave him a trip to North America, where he would live for eight months learning how to build canoes. The young man came and worked with Ron Frenette, who owns Canadian Canoes in Mississauga, Ontario. When Koji had learned the craft, he returned home and opened his own canoe-building business on the island of Hokkaido. Two other men who studied canoe building in North America have canoe businesses in the same area.

Frenette, who builds canoes, teaches how to build them, and puts together canoe-building kits, has shipped half a dozen canoes to Japan and others to people around the world. A man in Iceland ordered a canoe kit so he could go fishing; a man who lives on the Riviera ordered a canoe for decoration. A red wood and canvas canoe went to a professor

As the new millennium began, Henry John Billie, 77, of Big Cypress, Florida, was the last of the Seminole dugout canoe carvers. He learned the craft as a child, helping his father, who built canoes to transport fish and raccoon, alligator and otter hides to an Everglades trading post, where they obtained food and ammunition. Seminole dugouts were the main mode of transport through the Florida swamps until the Tamiami Trail was opened in 1928 and the craft of canoe building began to die. Billie hoped that younger Seminoles would begin apprenticing with him; however, cypress trees large enough for dugout carving have become scarce.

at Cambridge University in England, and another canoe went to a doctor in Sweden. Frenette's business is small, but he is one of hundreds of builders in the United States and Canada who are busier than ever meeting the increasing demand for canoes and kayaks around the world.

Japan is an example of the growth. It is estimated that there are more than 100,000 Japanese canoes and kayaks. The figure is remarkable when you consider the space problem in Japan. Someone once said that Japan boasts many world-class concert violinists but few pianists, because there is so little space in Japanese homes for pianos. There is just as little space for canoes.

The growth of canoeing and kayaking around the world can be attributed to many factors. People have more leisure time and there is a trend toward spending that time in healthy pursuits, many of them outdoors. There is also more disposable income to spend on equipment. And the addition of canoe and kayak slalom events to the Olympics in the early 1990s has promoted interest in racing and adventure paddling. Between 40 and 50 countries now compete in Olympic canoe and kayak events.

North America remains the spiritual home and statistical center for paddling. As the new century opened, more than 26 million North Americans participated in paddle sports, according to statistics from the Sporting Goods Manufacturers Association of the U.S. and Industry Canada. Canoeing and

One of the most unusual canoe competitions in the world is the annual ice canoe race at the Carnival in Quebec City. Teams race their canoes across water and ice flows in the St. Lawrence River. (Left) Sport canoeing continued its steady climb in popularity throughout the 1990s.

kayaking during the 1990s were consistently listed among the top five growth sports of the continent. Canadian and U.S. canoe associations that promote racing, the recreational canoe associations, and manufacturing groups all report more people participating in paddle sports. Kayaking, particularly sea kayaking and tour kayaking, is experiencing explosive growth. In 1998 there were between 3.5 and 4 million kayakers in North America.

Statistics show that in 1999 more than 3 million North Americans owned canoes, kayaks, or rowboats. U.S. sales of canoes in 1999 were 121,000 with a value of US$64 million, up from 103,000 valued at US$61 million in 1997. Ten years earlier, canoe sales in the U.S. were US$38 million.

Buying Your Own Canoe

The first step in buying a canoe is to figure out what you plan to do with it. Will you use it for fishing and camping? Will you canoe on big lakes, rivers with rapids, or quiet ponds? Do you plan to portage? Will you most often paddle alone? The answers to these questions help determine the length and width of canoe and the hull shape you need.

Width: A canoe's width is an important factor in speed and stability. The wider the canoe, the more bottom there is to create drag across the water. Drag slows speed, thereby increasing the effort needed to paddle. Wider canoes are more stable, however, and can carry more gear.

Length: Obviously, the longer the canoe, the more people it will carry. Longer canoes generally travel faster and track more easily, but more length means more bottom touching the surface, and thus more effort required to paddle.

Rocker: The line running from bow to stern along the bottom of a canoe is called the keel line. The amount that this line curves upward at the ends is called rocker. A lot of rocker means less bottom against the water and therefore better maneuverability, but it is harder to paddle the canoe straight. Big lake canoes have almost no rocker, making them easy to

Canoes should be selected not only for smooth handling on the water but also for ease of portaging.

Portaging can lead to serious injury if not done properly. Learning how to carry a canoe and safe portaging practices are a vital part of canoeing.

paddle in a straight line over long distances. River canoes have more rocker, making them easy to turn quickly.

Hull shape: Flat-bottom canoes don't tip as easily. They feel more stable and provide a level of comfort when canoeing for a specific reason, such as fishing. V-shaped hulls tend to feel tippier, although they are not necessarily so (depending on the other characteristics of the canoe). V shapes usually are faster and easier to turn. The sides of a canoe can differ as well. A canoe side that rises straight to the gunwales is called plumb. One that flares outward is called flared, and one that turns inward is called tumblehome. Each has to be considered an important part of the overall approach to the canoe. For instance, a flared side tends to hold back wave splash but is more awkward to paddle, because the paddler must reach further out over the side.

Keels: A keel is a strip that runs along the middle of a watercraft's bottom. In sailboats the keel creates stability, among other things, to prevent capsizing. Somewhere in the mists of history a misconception developed about keels and their effect on canoe performance. Keels are not needed on most canoes. Originally, a wood or metal keel strip was put on canvas or wood-strip canoes to protect the bottom. Fiberglass canoes often have one or more keels, but these are designed mainly to give stiffness to the bottom.

Materials: There are many choices of materials and many reasons for selecting one or another. Aluminum is light and will take much abuse, but aluminum canoes are noisy; you can hear a paddle strike a gunwale clear across a small lake. Traditional canvas and cedar and cedar-strip canoes can be works of art. They are expensive and require a reasonable level of care in handling. Fiberglass canoes have become the most popular because they are durable and have a wider range of affordability. There are so many designs and differences in quality of fiberglass canoes that buying one requires a fair amount of study and testing, if possible. There are probably more chances of poor design in fiberglass canoes than in any of the other categories. Kevlar and other specialty cloth can be super light, making excellent canoes, but they are expensive. Canoes made of ABS and other plastics have become popular for their ruggedness. They are almost indestructible but can be heavier than other materials.

Winter canoeing provides a different perspective on the wilderness. It can be a dangerous pastime, however, and should be undertaken only by experienced canoeists.

Choosing the Paddle

The paddle, as first invented, was a simple tool. Modern materials and different types of canoeing have made it more complicated. There are now curved paddles, fiberglass paddles, and paddles made from aluminum filled with plastic. There are only two basic paddles, however: the single blade and the double blade, used for kayaking.

Blade shapes and sizes vary for different types of use. The single paddle has two main grips, the pear grip and the T-grip. The latter is most often used in whitewater because it allows a better grip. The pear grip is used on traditional canoe paddles in which the top of the paddle is held between the palm and fingers.

The traditional canoe paddle is roughly 5½ feet (1.7 m) long with a blade about 5 inches (13 cm) wide. Paddles made of softwood, such as spruce, are light but do not have the durability of heavier hardwood paddles made of maple, beech, or ash. In addition, hardwood can be feathered to give the paddle blade a fine edge.

During an hour of canoeing a person will make 1,500 to 1,800 strokes, so paddle selection requires some thought. A poor choice can make for a frustrating day on the water. New paddlers tend to buy paddles that are too long, thinking that length will give them power. A long paddle tends to force the upper hand up much too high. Experienced canoeists often choose short paddles with narrow blades that produce a smoother stroke with the least effort.

Using Your Canoe

One of the beauties of canoeing is that it can be done simply by entering the canoe (carefully) and starting to paddle. The strokes are simple: pull the paddle through the water bow to stern to travel forwards; push the paddle stern to bow to move backwards. Obviously, canoeing involves much more skill than that. The point is, however, that a complete novice can do it immediately and then acquire further skills through experience or instruction. The actual mechanics of canoeing can be learned quickly; the knowledge and skills required for canoe travel—handling different waters, portaging, living safely and comfortably in the outdoors—require study, coaching, and experience.

Building Your Own Canoe

It has never been easier to build your own canoe. There are courses, workshops, canoe-building kits. The choice of materials is wide and tools are sophisticated. If you don't have room to build it at home, there are places where you can go to build it and, if needed, to get some instruction at the same time. Most libraries have books on canoe design and building. The Internet holds a wealth of information and contacts with canoe-building groups. Any store that sells canoeing equipment likely has contacts to help you get involved in building.

Books on Canoeing

Bark Canoes and Skin Boats of America (Adney/Chappelle).
The acknowledged expert book on canoes.
Birch Bark Canoe (David Gidmark). Interesting story of a
man who goes to live with the Algonquins in Quebec and
learns to build birch-bark canoes.
Paddle to the Sea (Holling C. Holling). For children.
Path of the Paddle and *Song of the Paddle* (Key Porter Books,
Bill Mason).
Cradle to Canoe: Camping and Canoeing with Children (Rolf
and Debra Kraiker).

Some Canoe Web Sites

American Canoe Association
http://www.acanet.org/acanet.htm
Canadian Canoe Association
http://www.openface.ca/paddle/index.html
Canadian Canoe Museum
http://www.canoemuseum.net/index.htm
Canadian Recreational Canoeing Association
http://www.crca.ca/CRCACore.cfm
Canoe and Kayak Ring
http://www.webcre8.com/canoe/listing.html

Olympic Canoe/Kayak

    http://www.Olympics.com/eng/sports/

Sigurd Olson Web Site

    http://www.uwm.edu/Dept/JMC/Olson/profile.htm

U.S. Canoe Association

    http://usca-canoe-kayak.org

Variety of Links

    http://www.canoe.ca/AllAboutCanoes/canoe_links.html

Wooden Canoe Heritage Association

    http://www.wcha.org/index.html